Believe In Yourself

I0481334

Good Vibes Coloring Book
By Lassie Honey

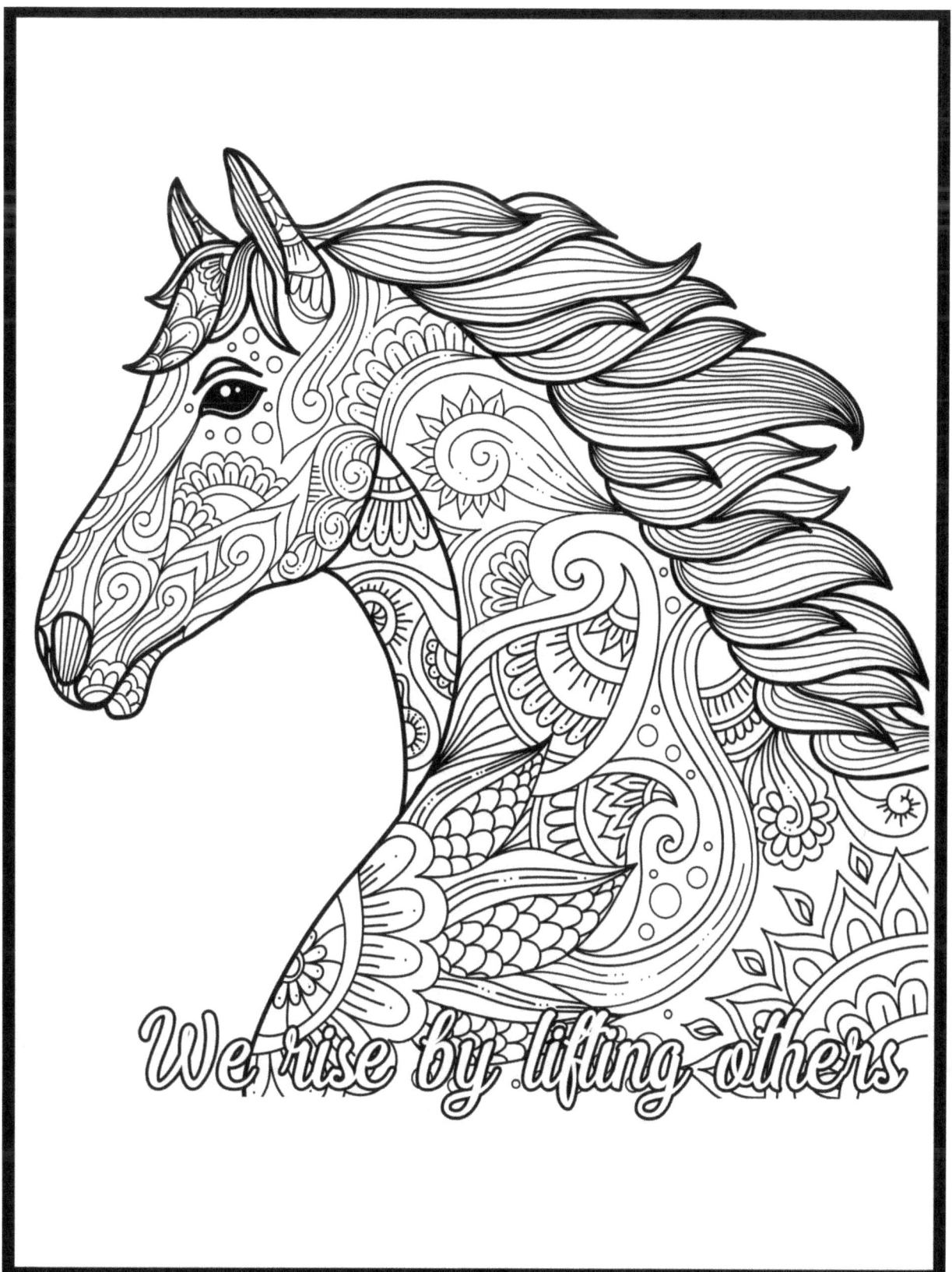

We rise by lifting others

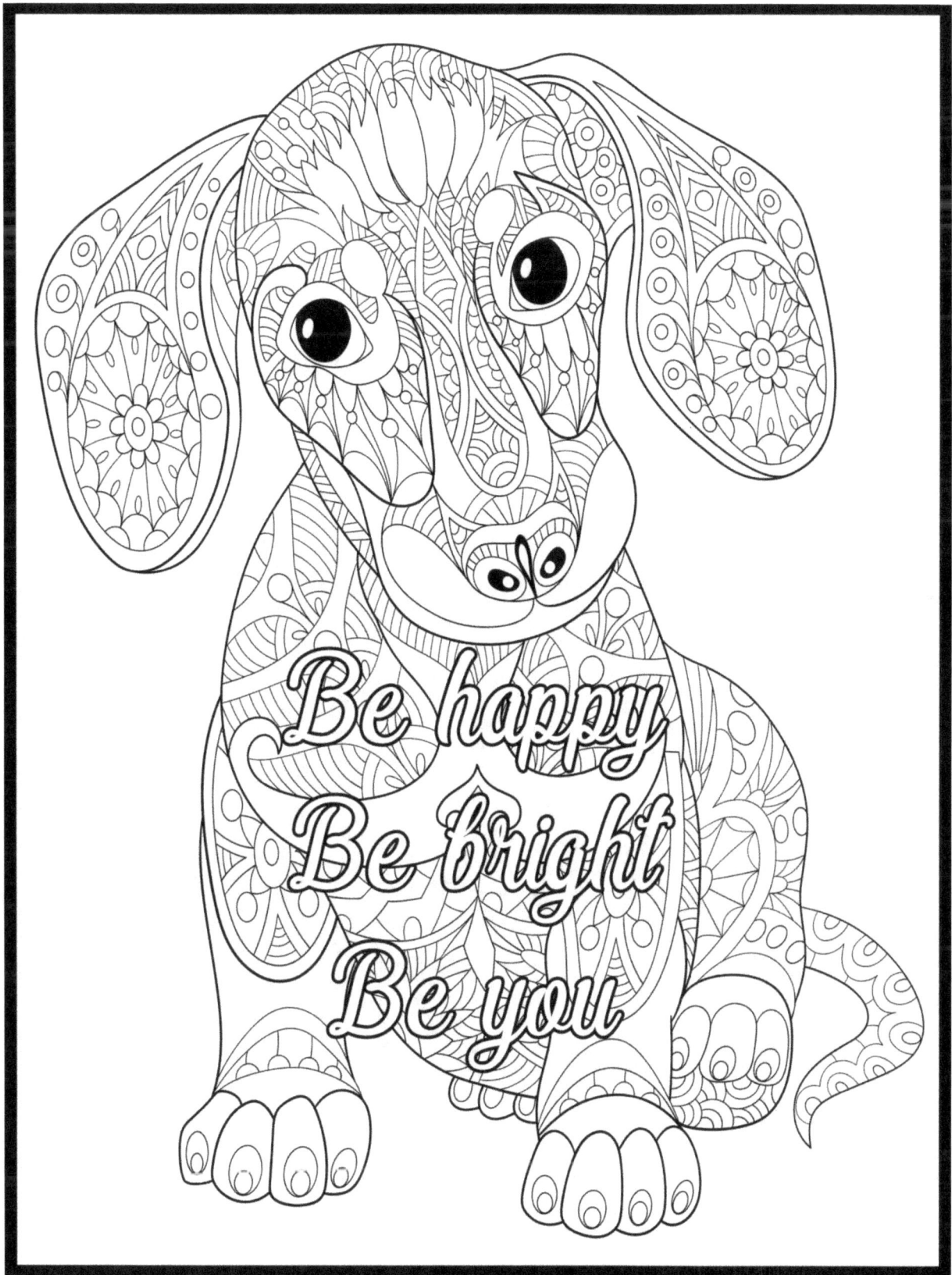

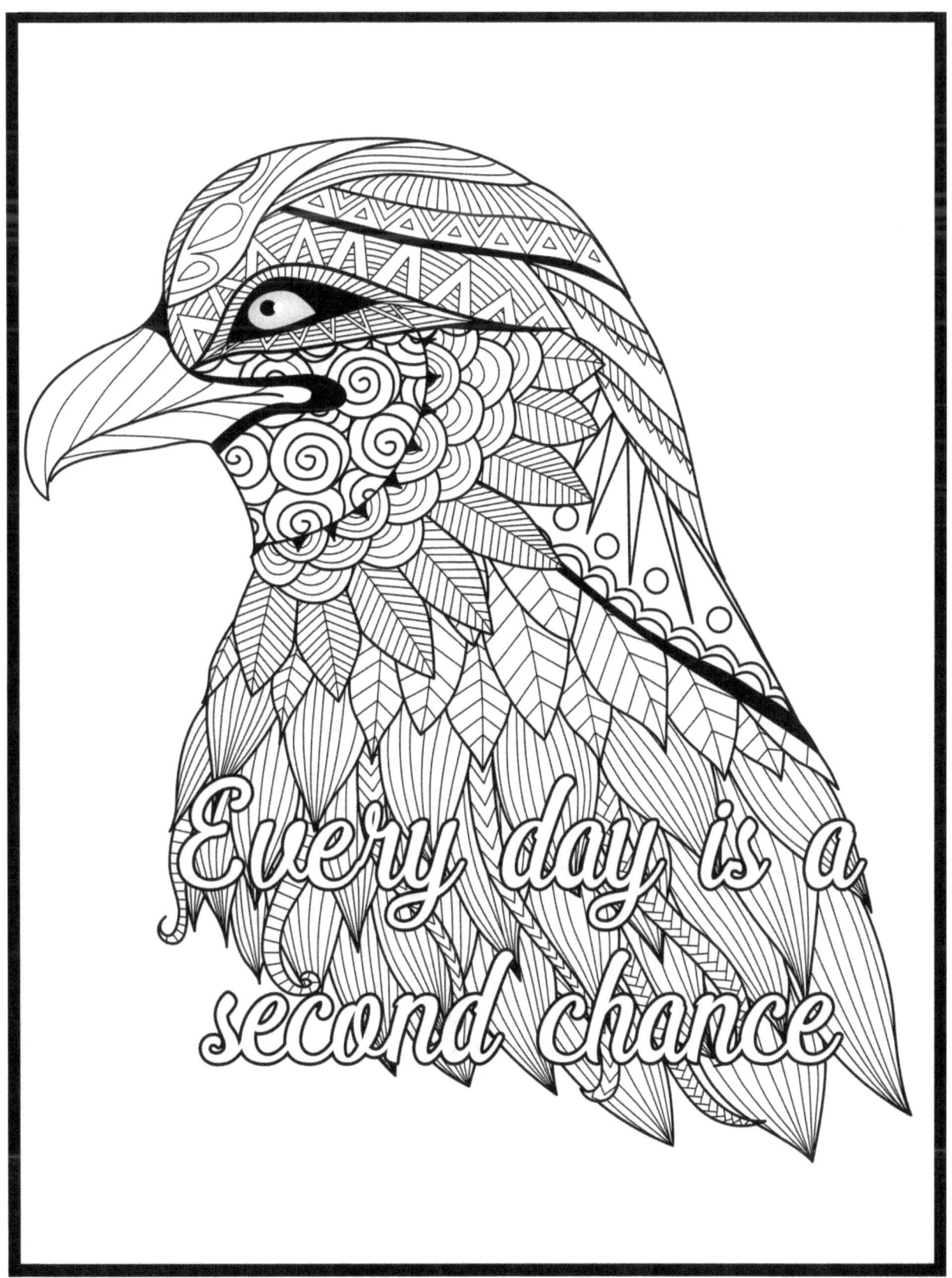

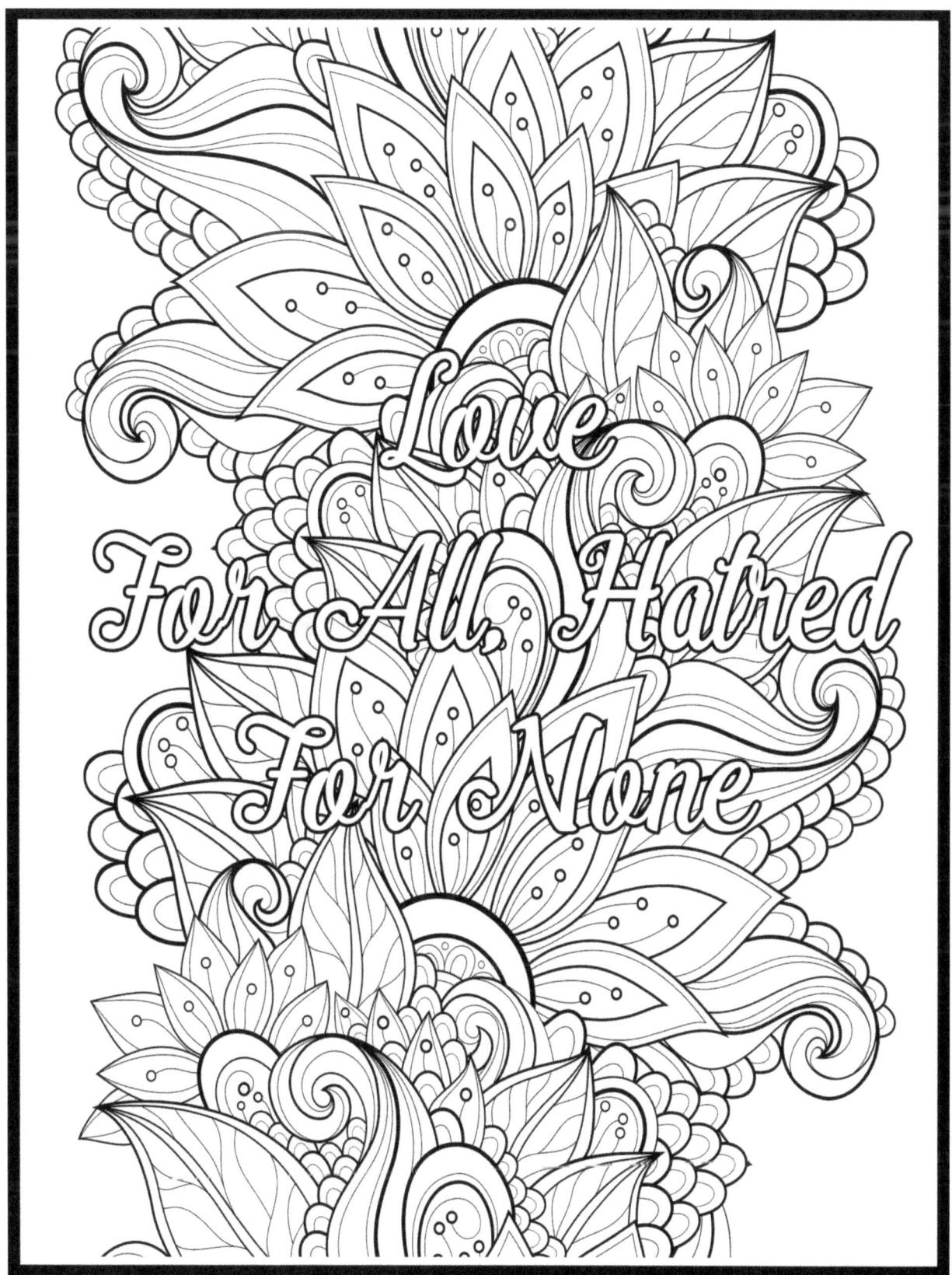

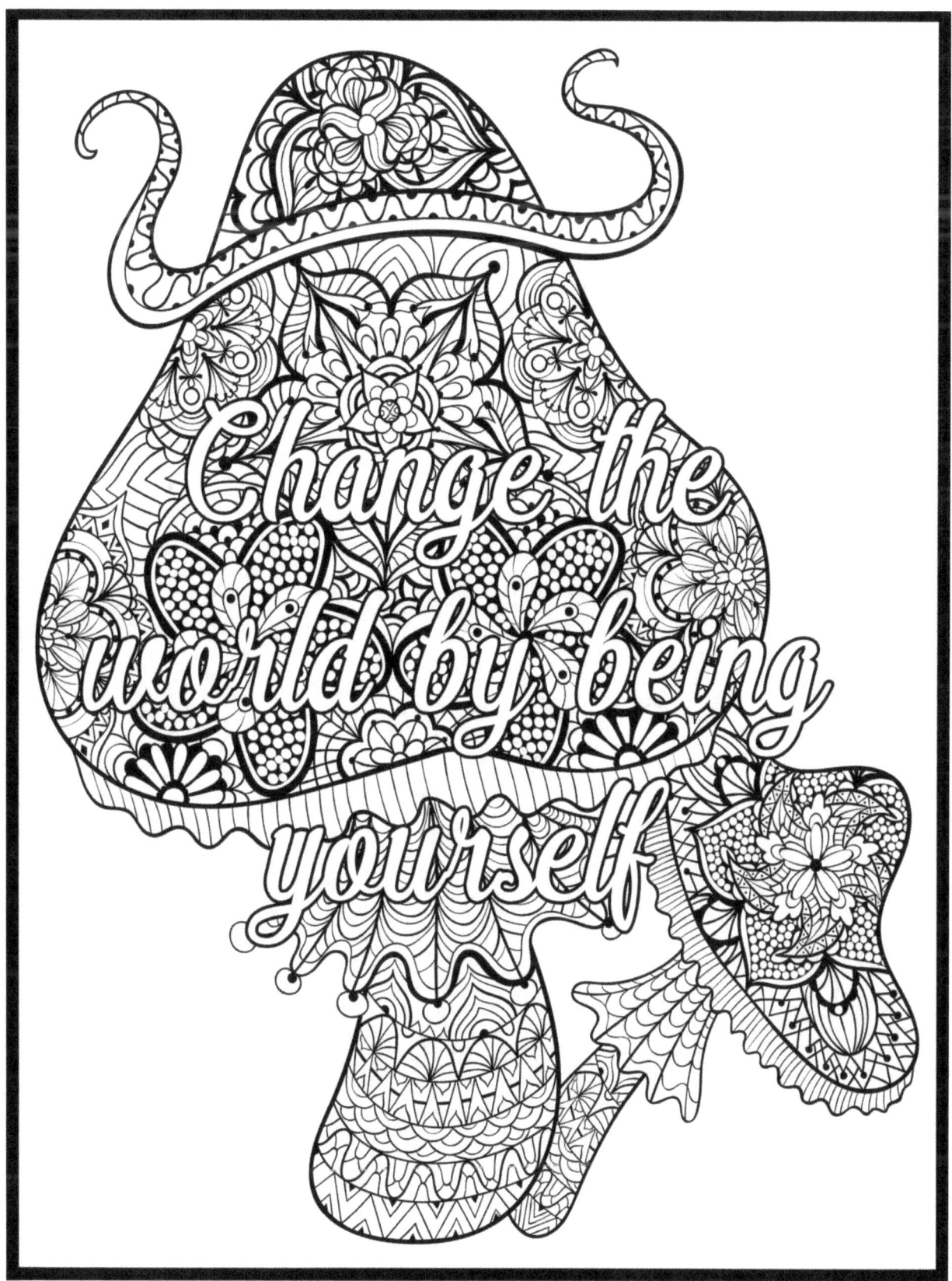

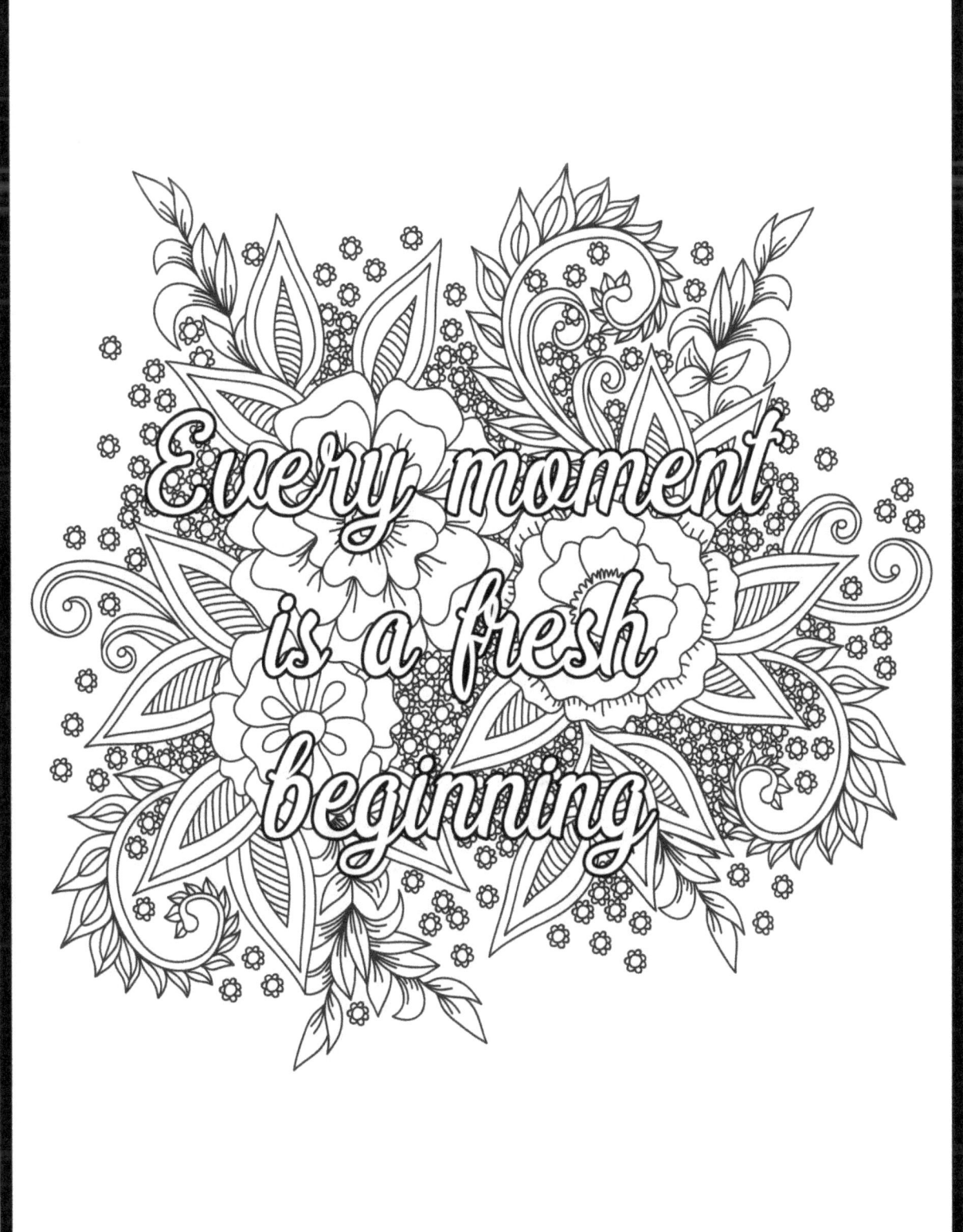

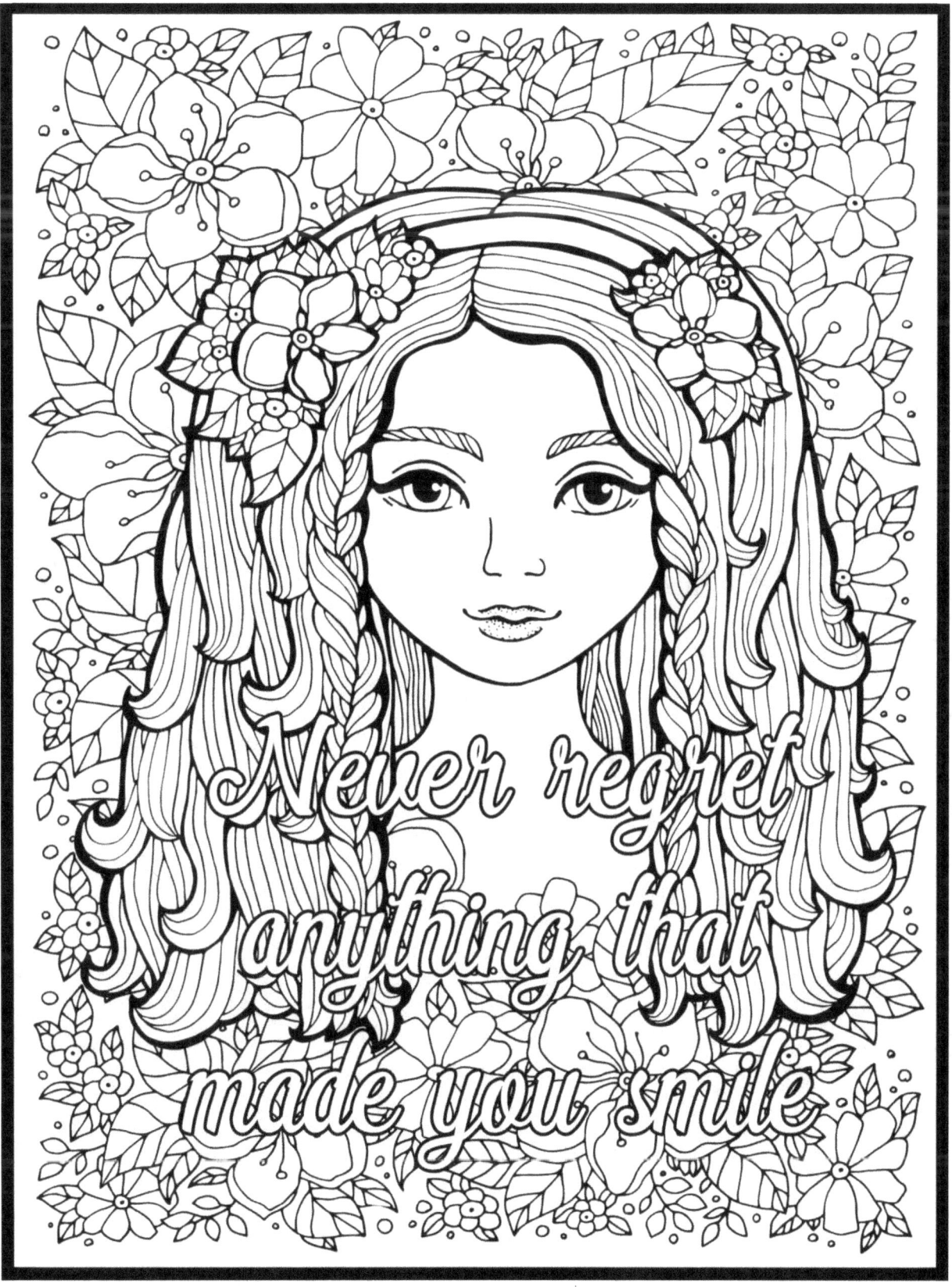

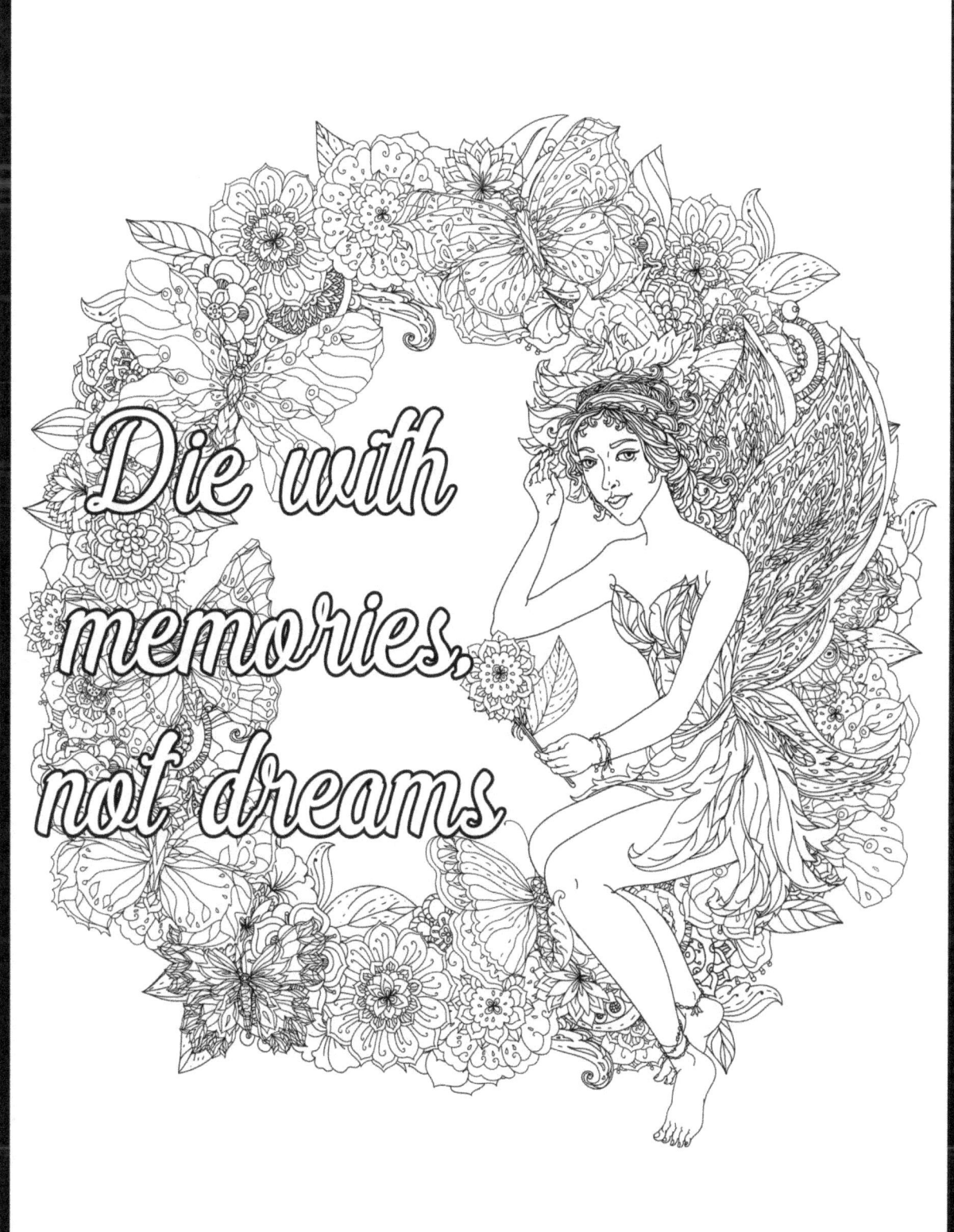

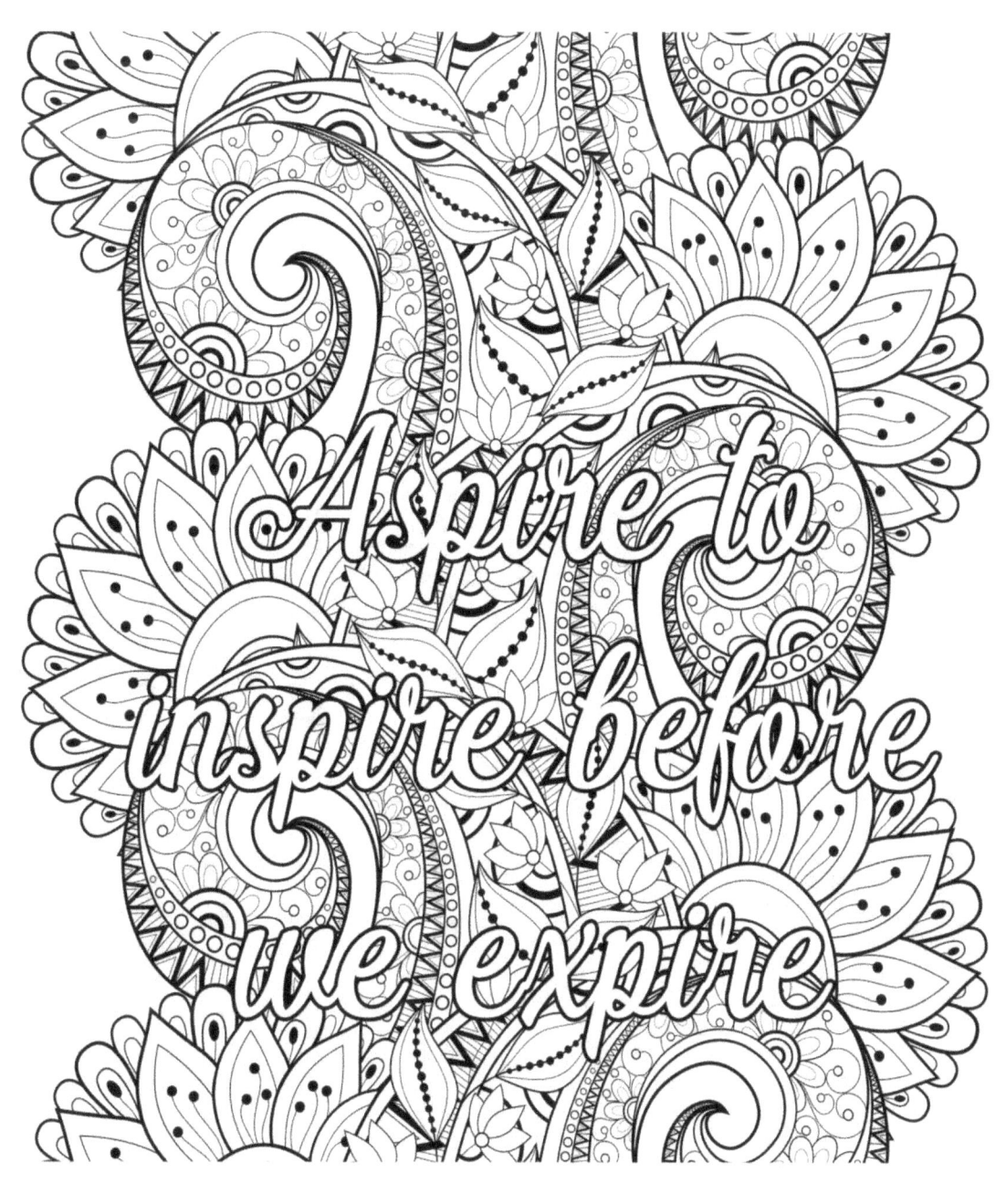

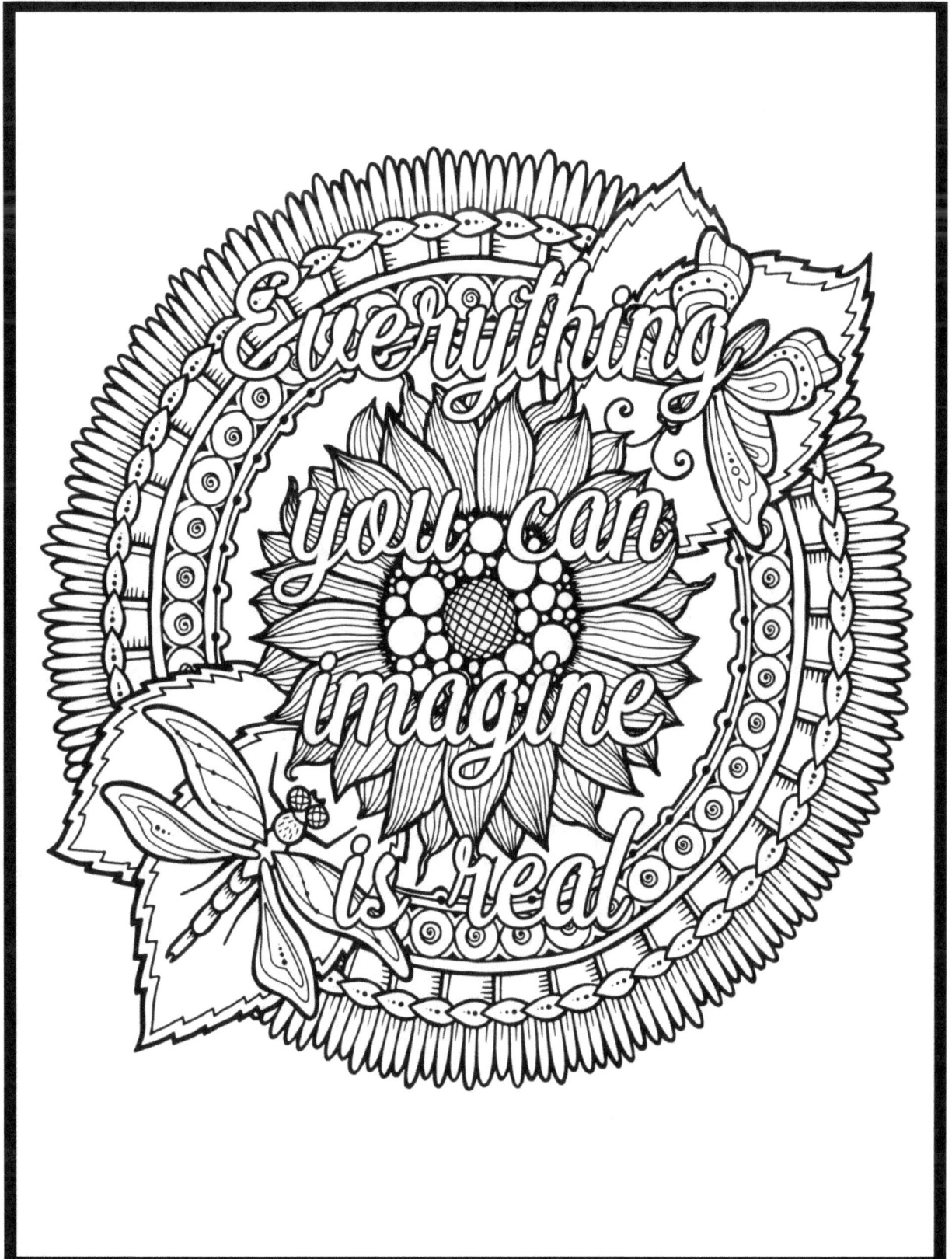

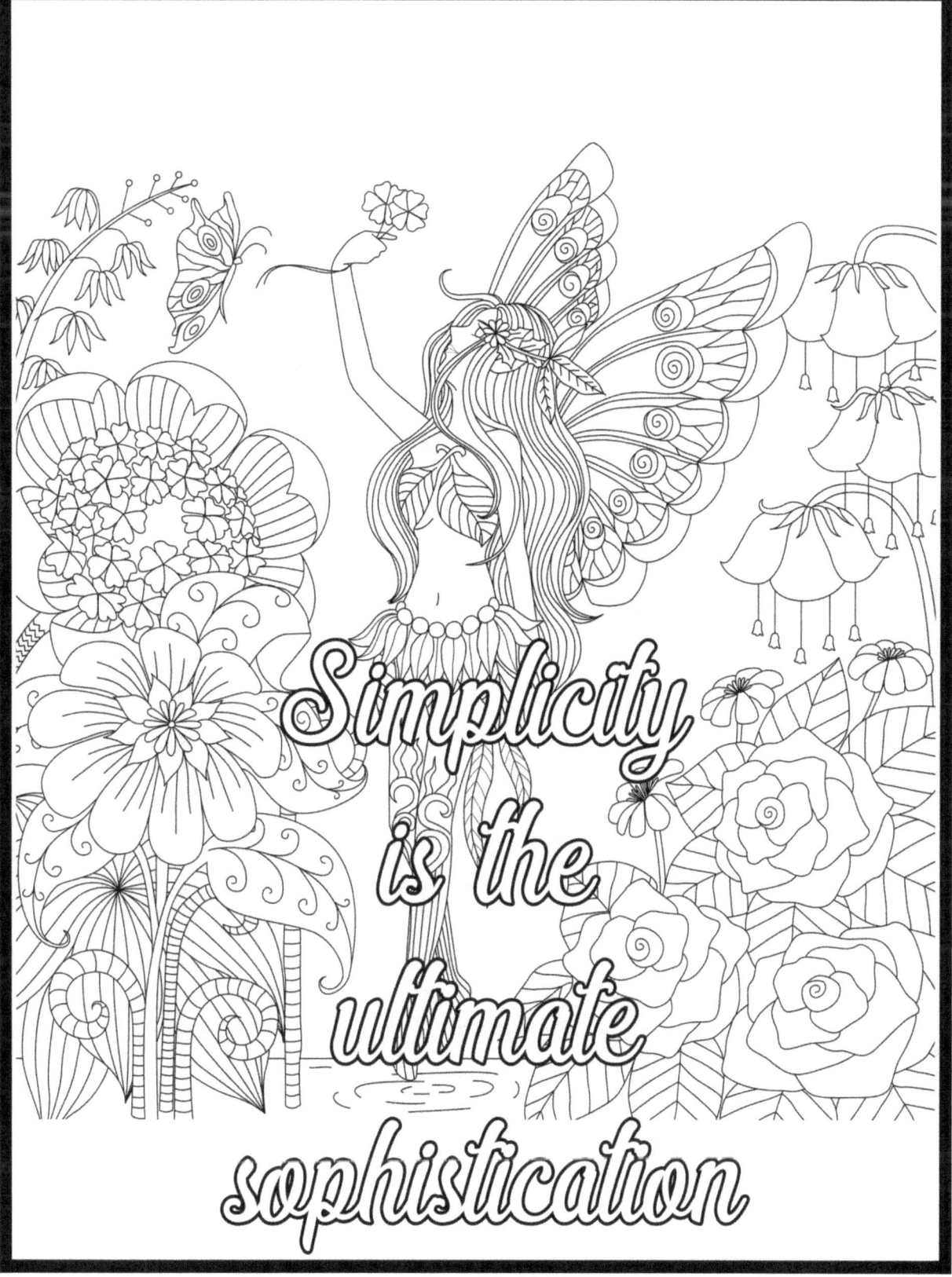

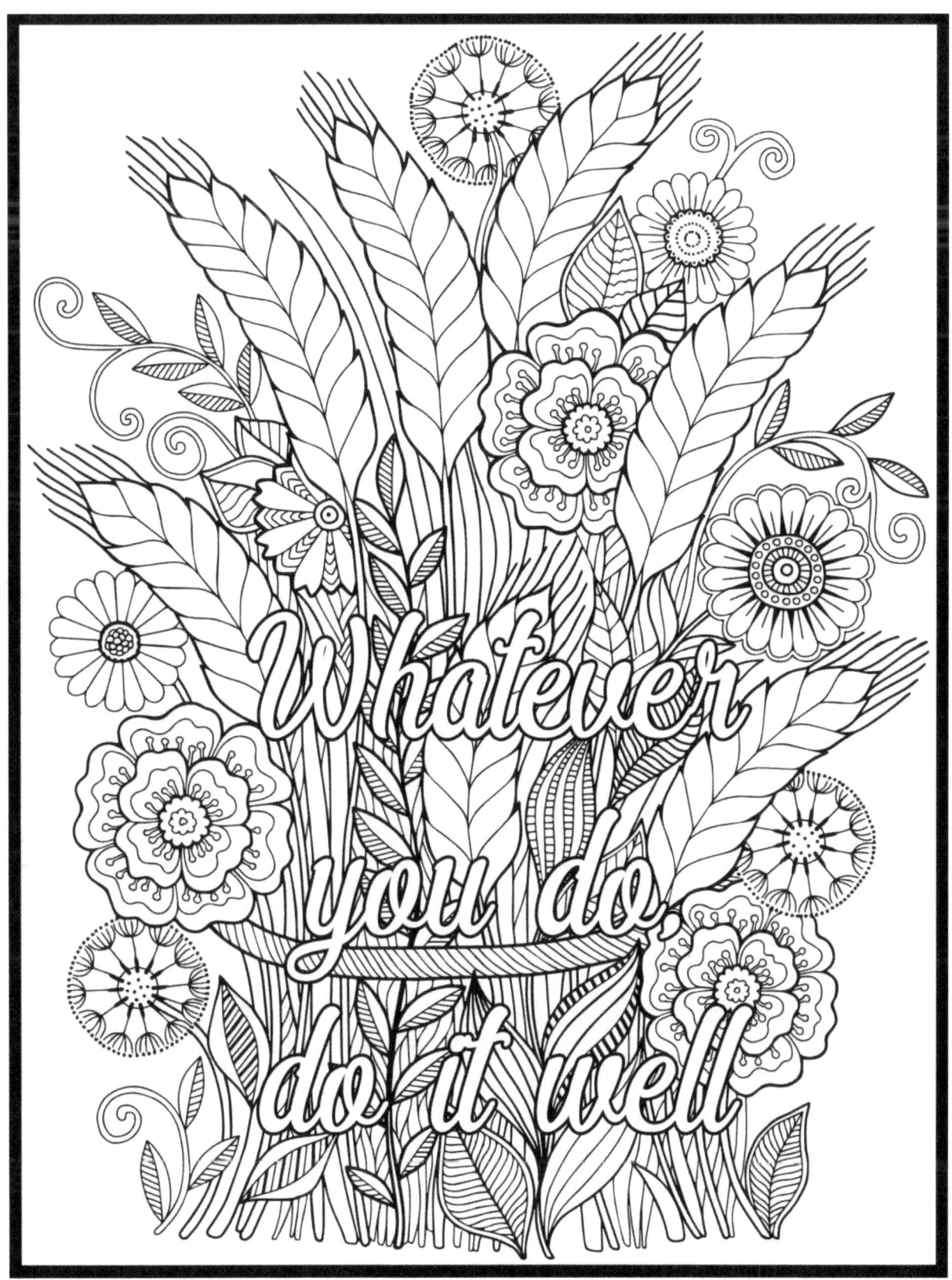

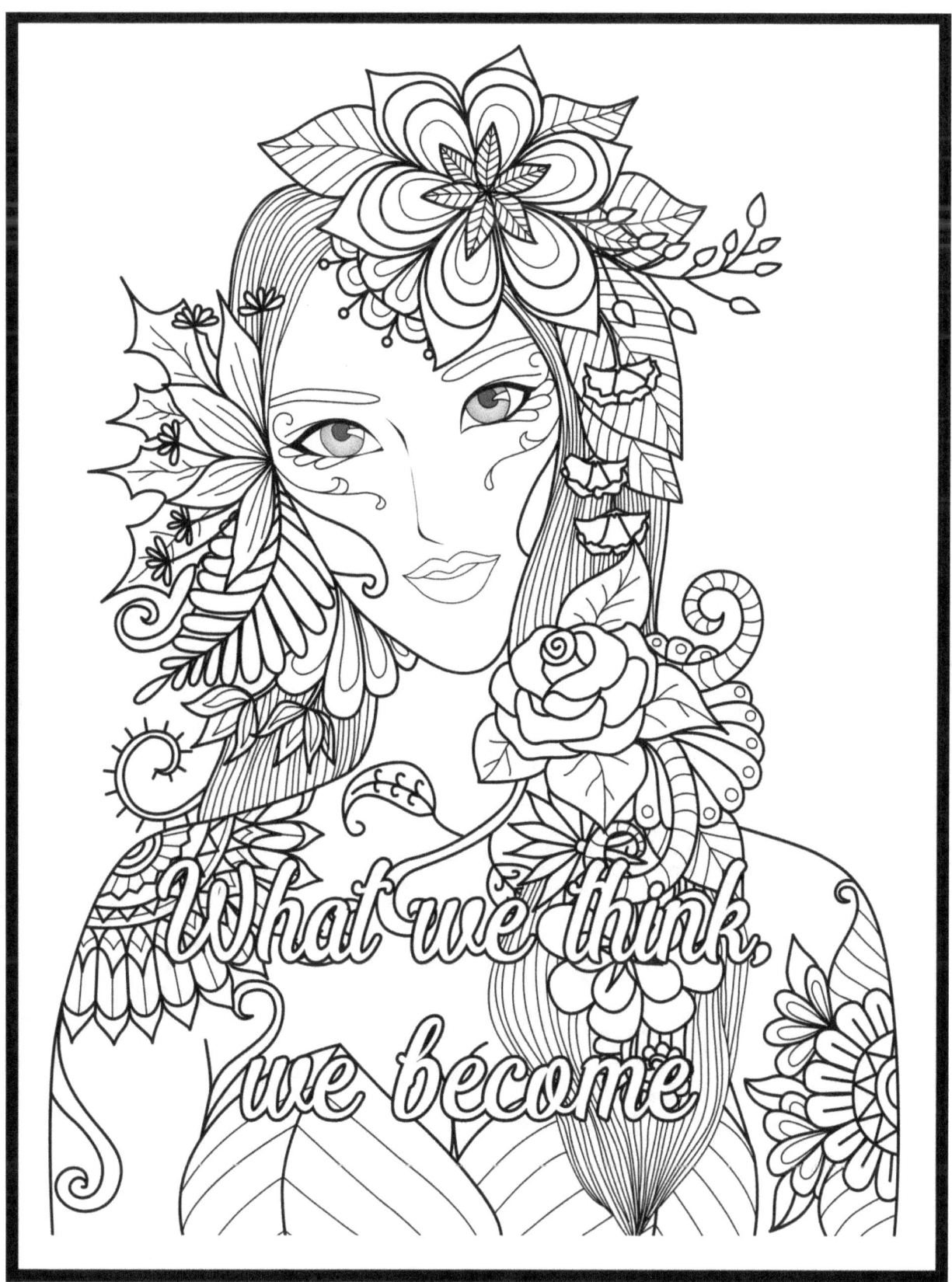

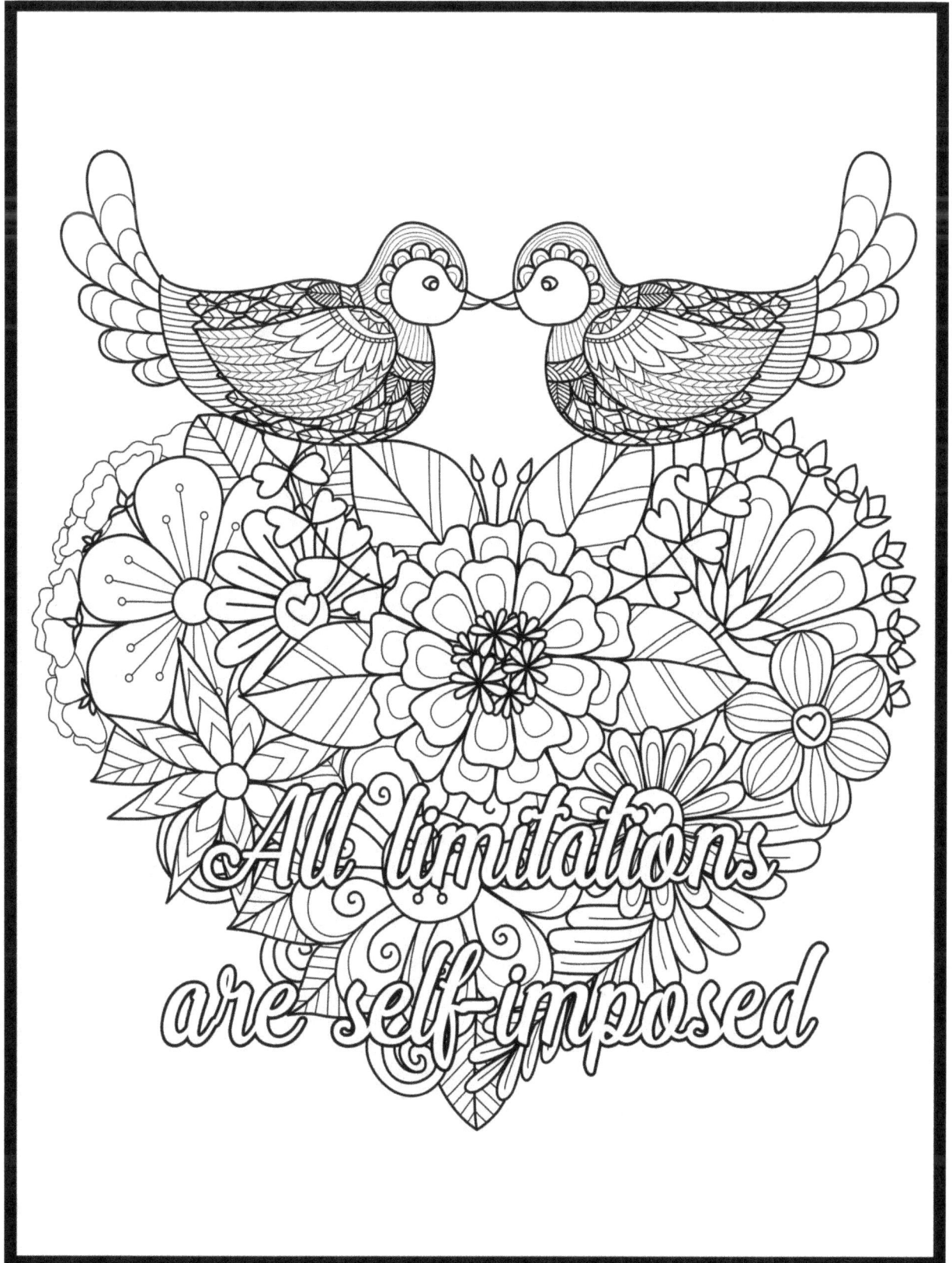

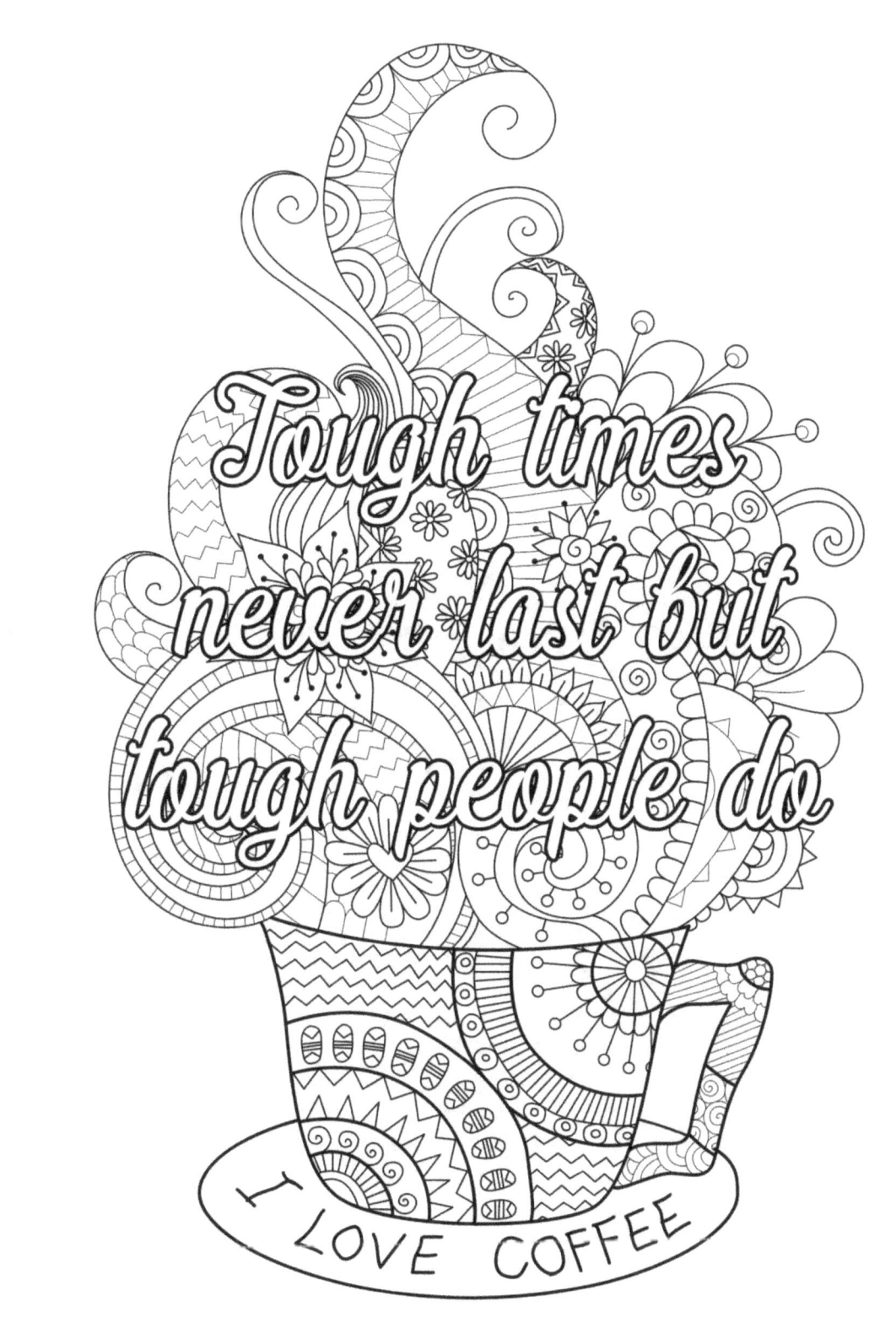

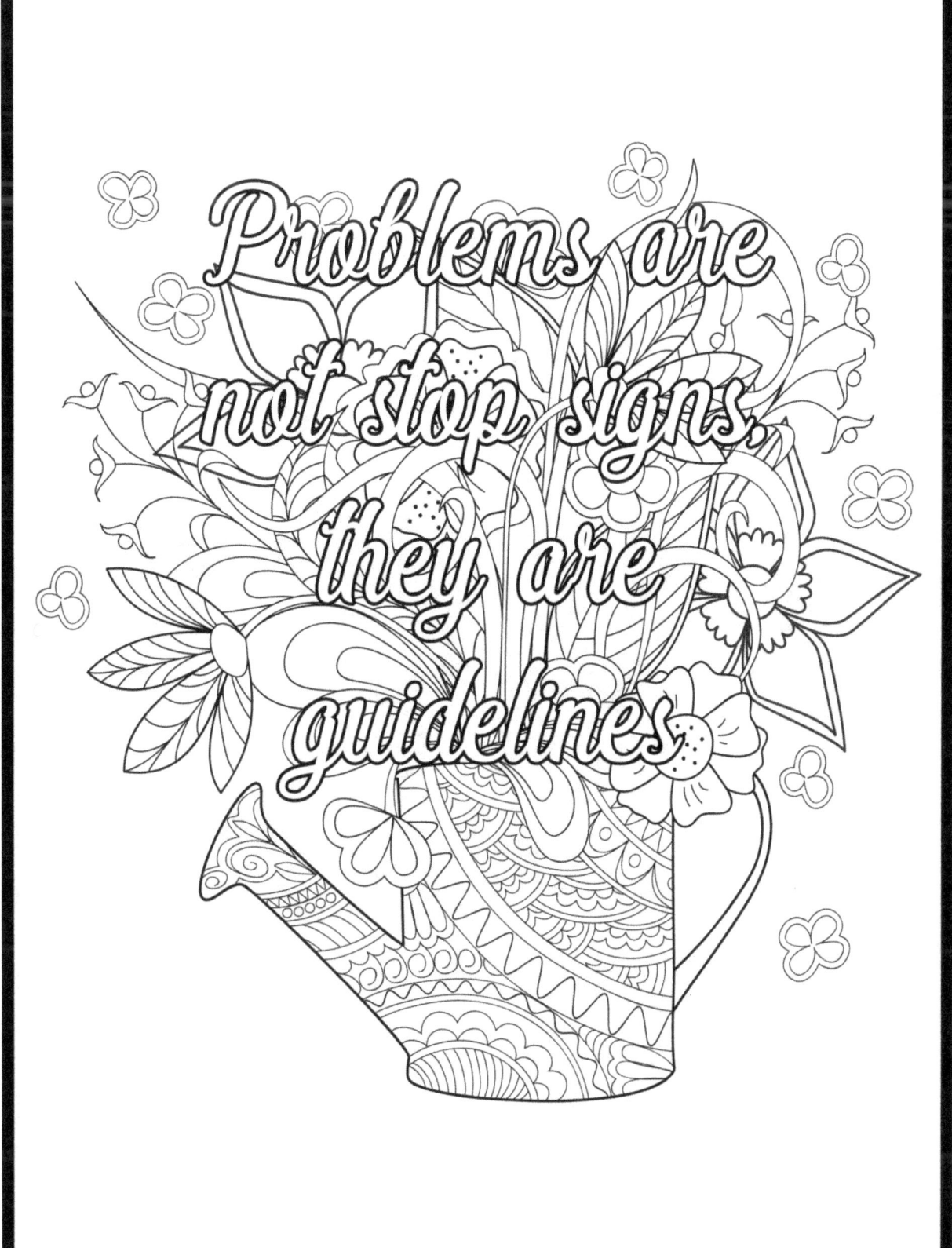

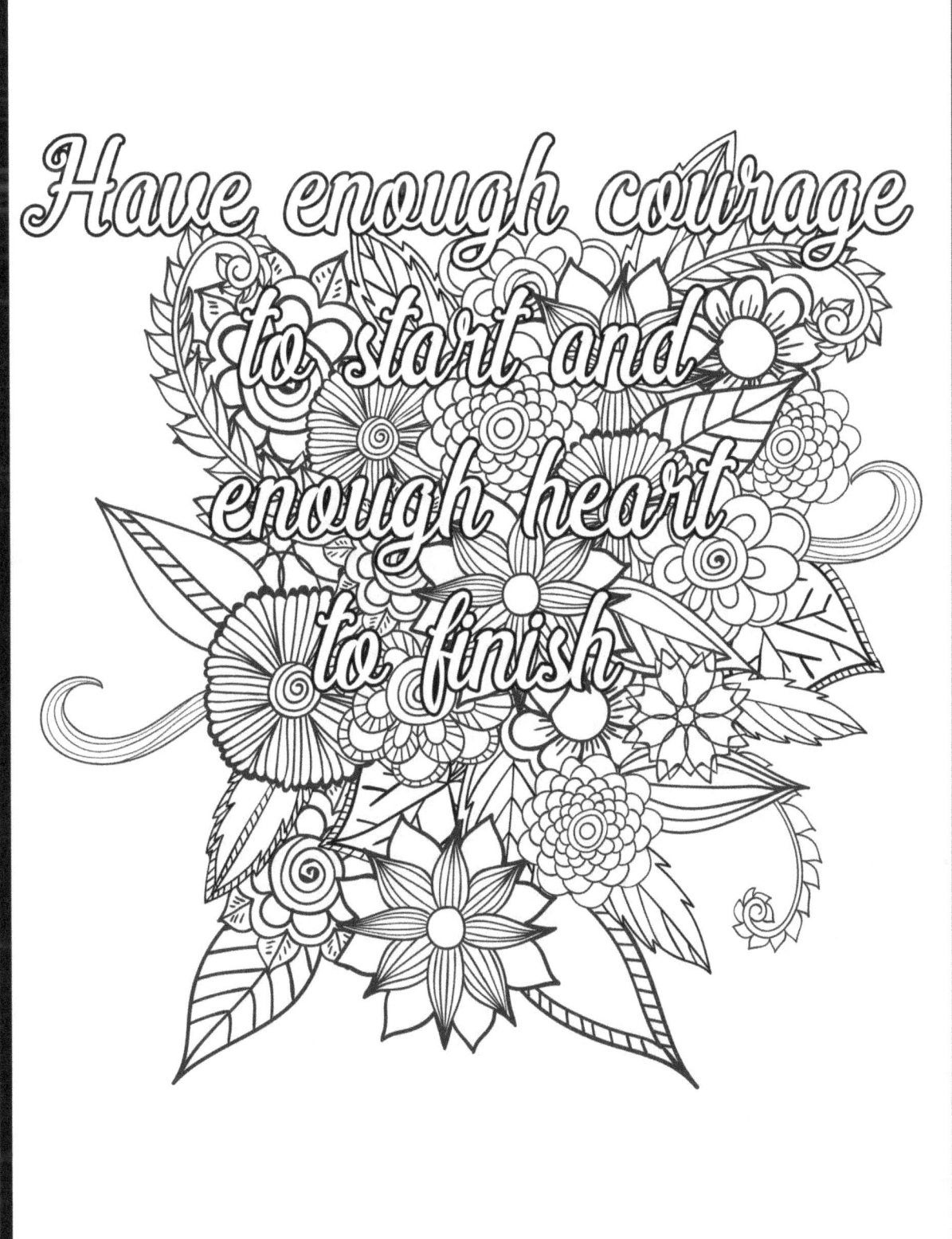

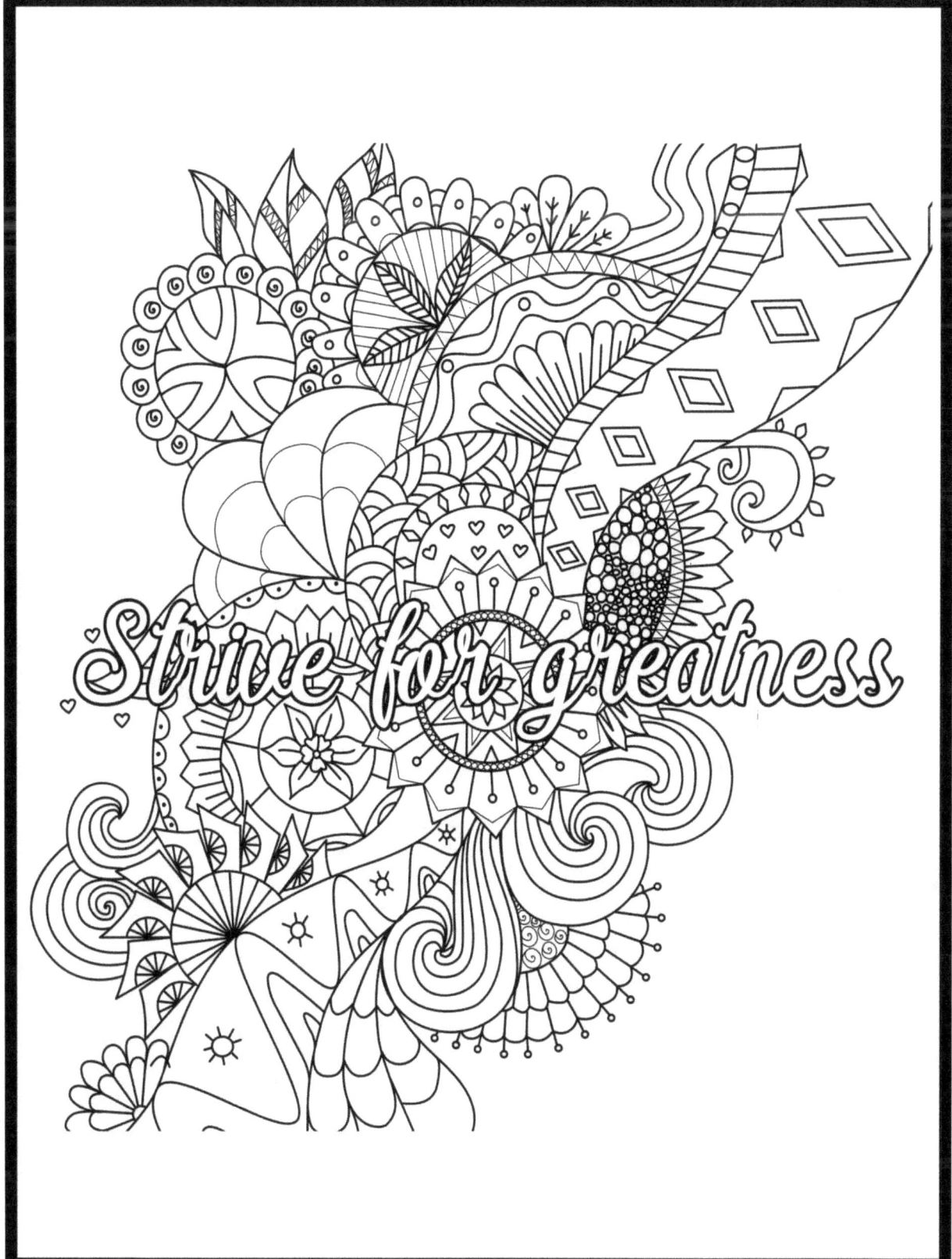

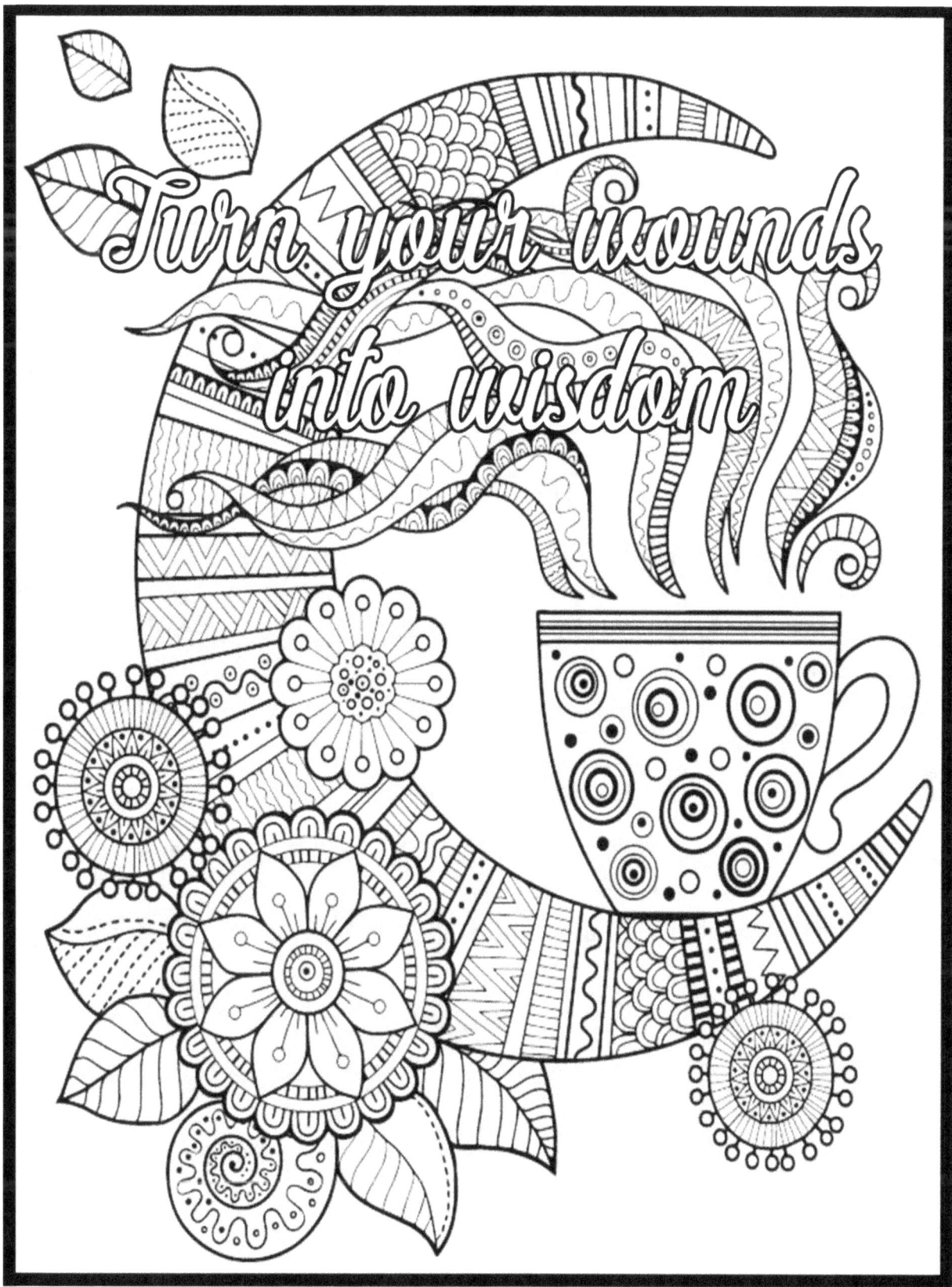

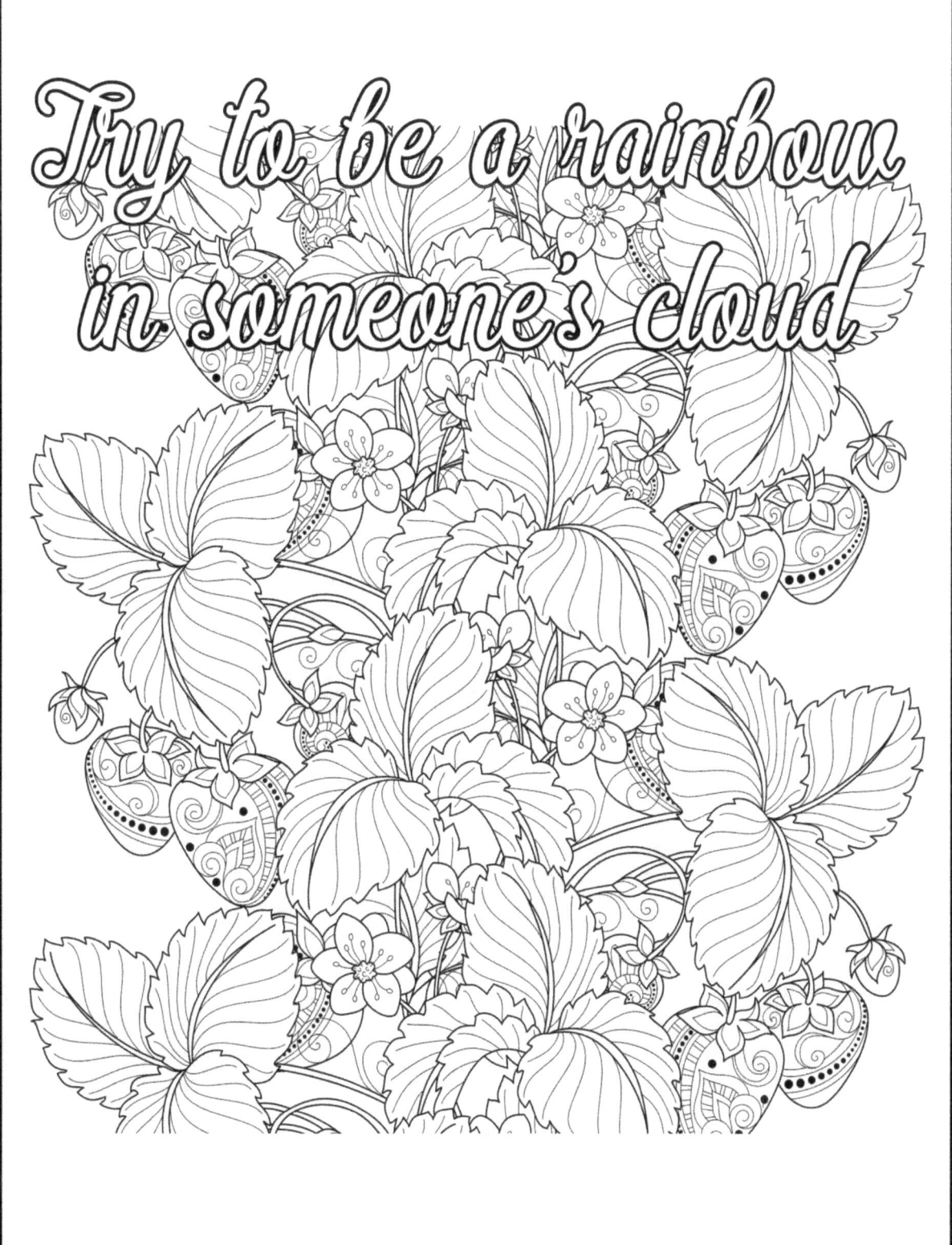

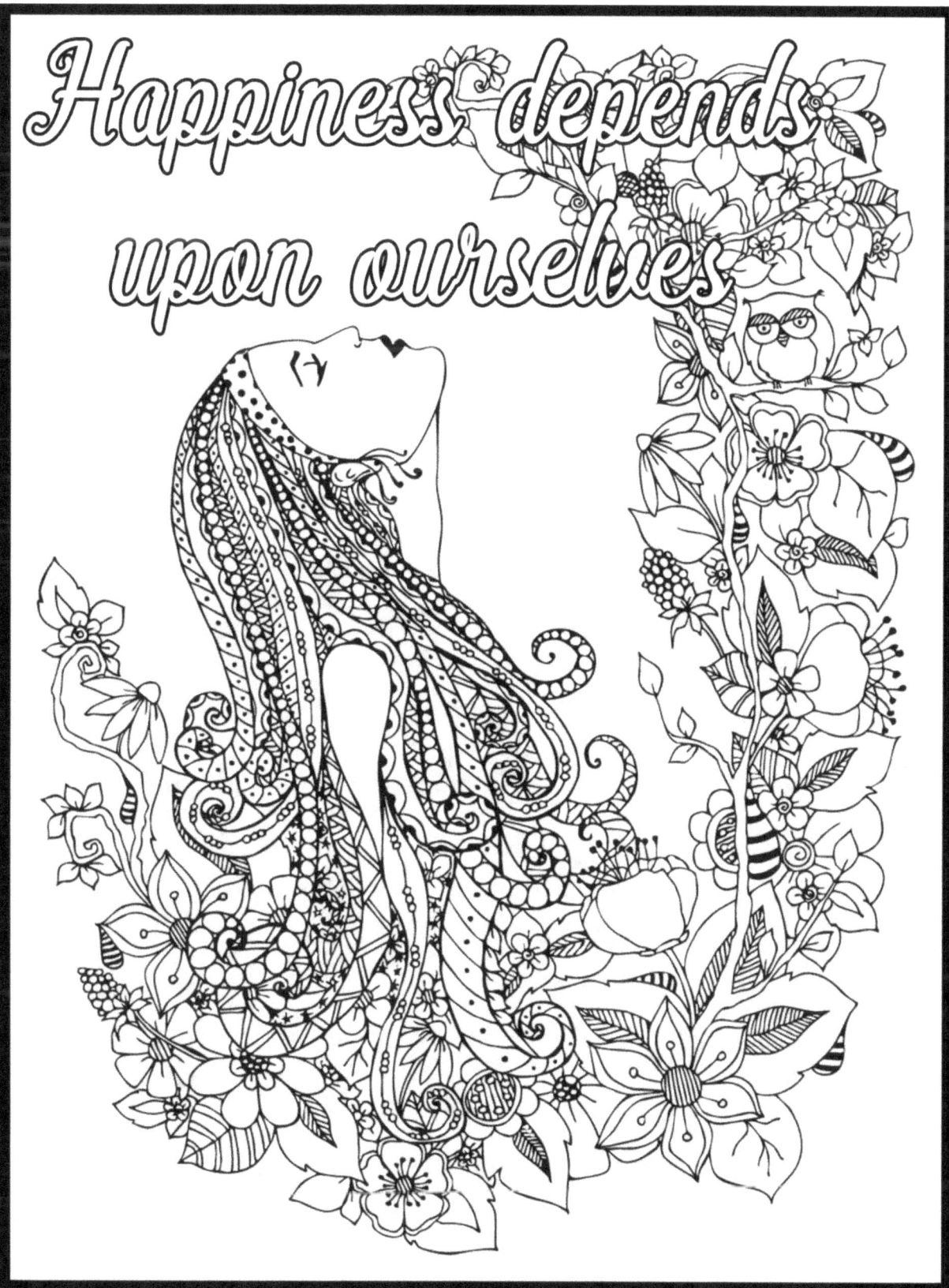

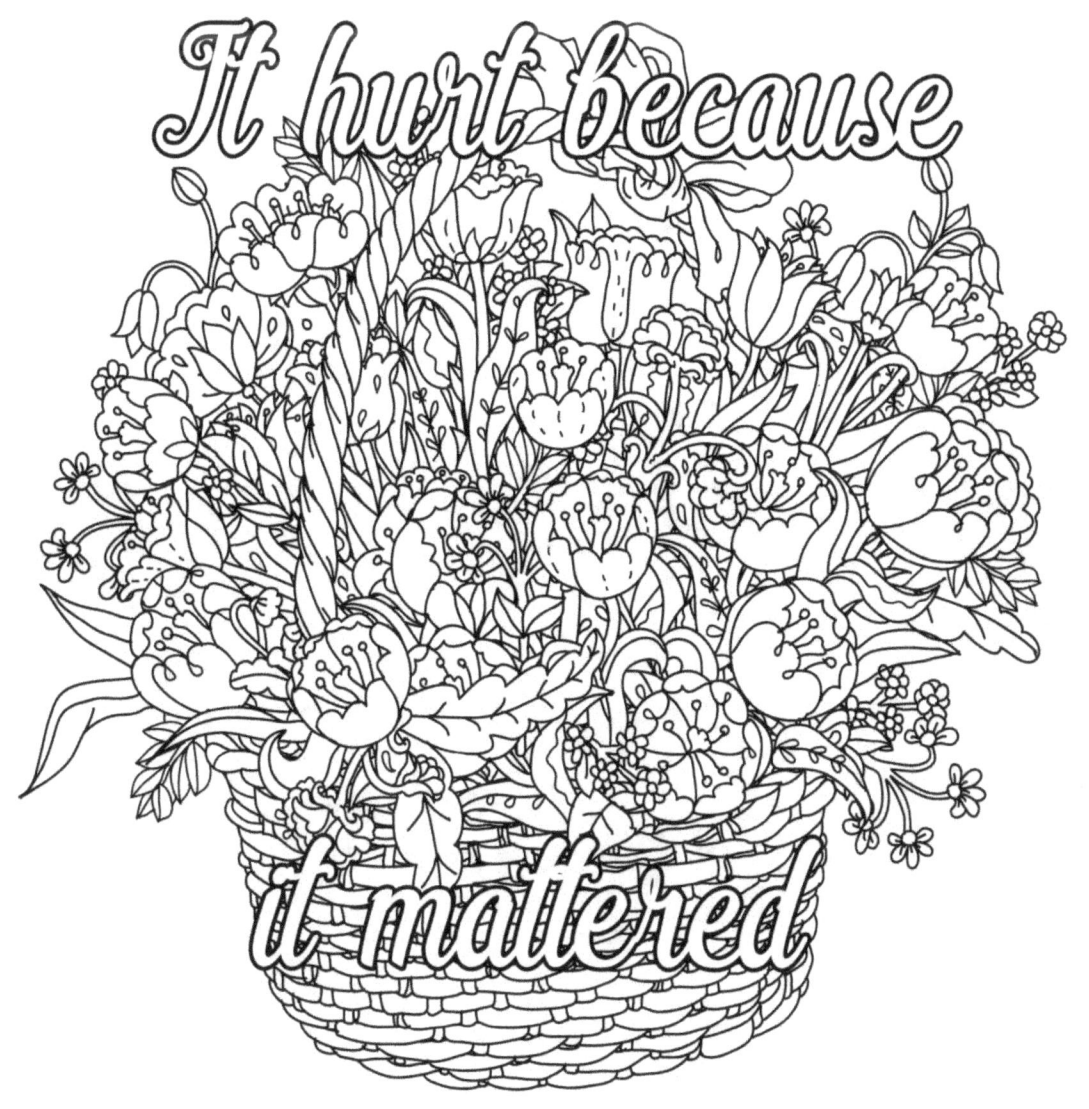

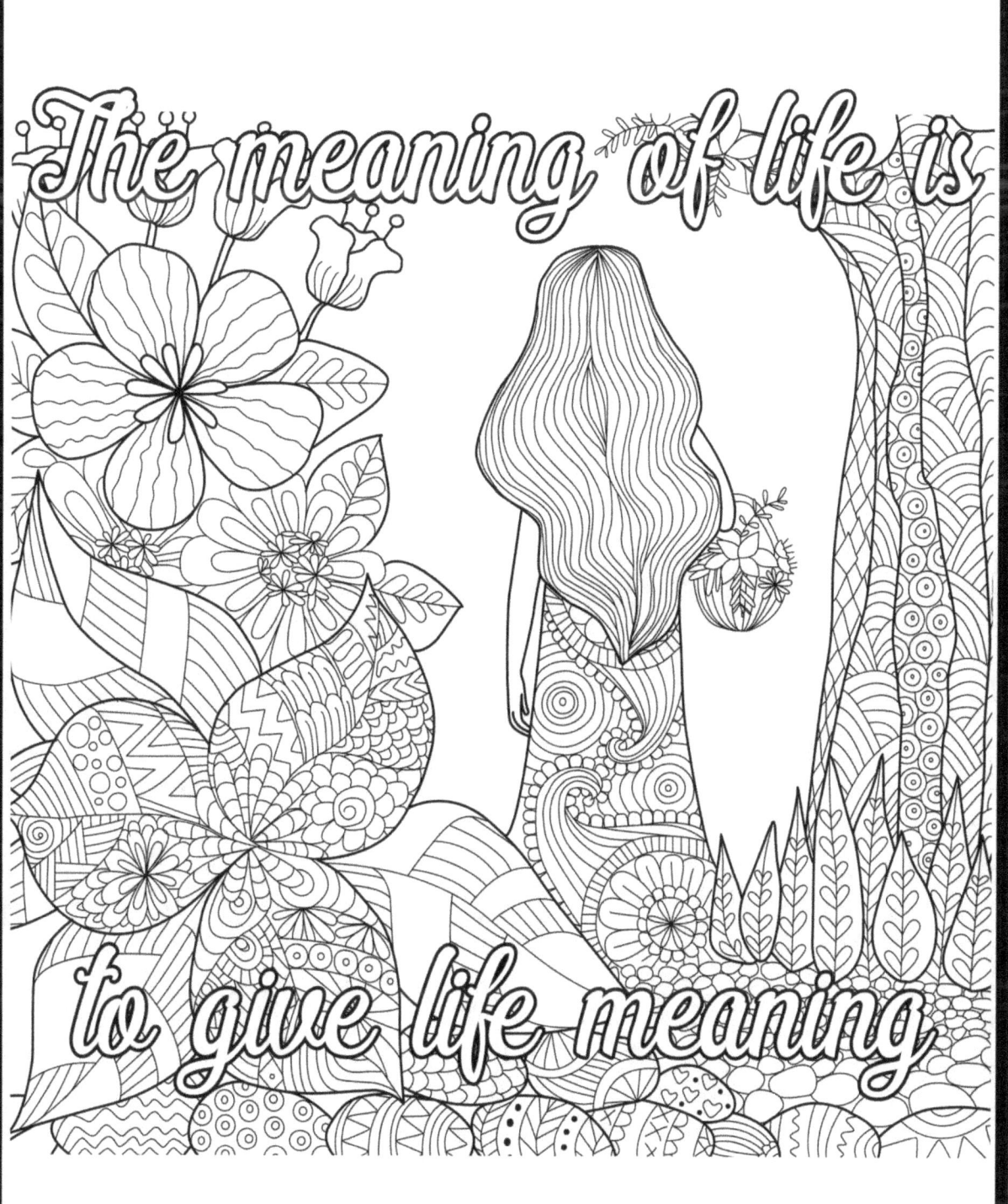

Be yourself

everyone else

is already taken

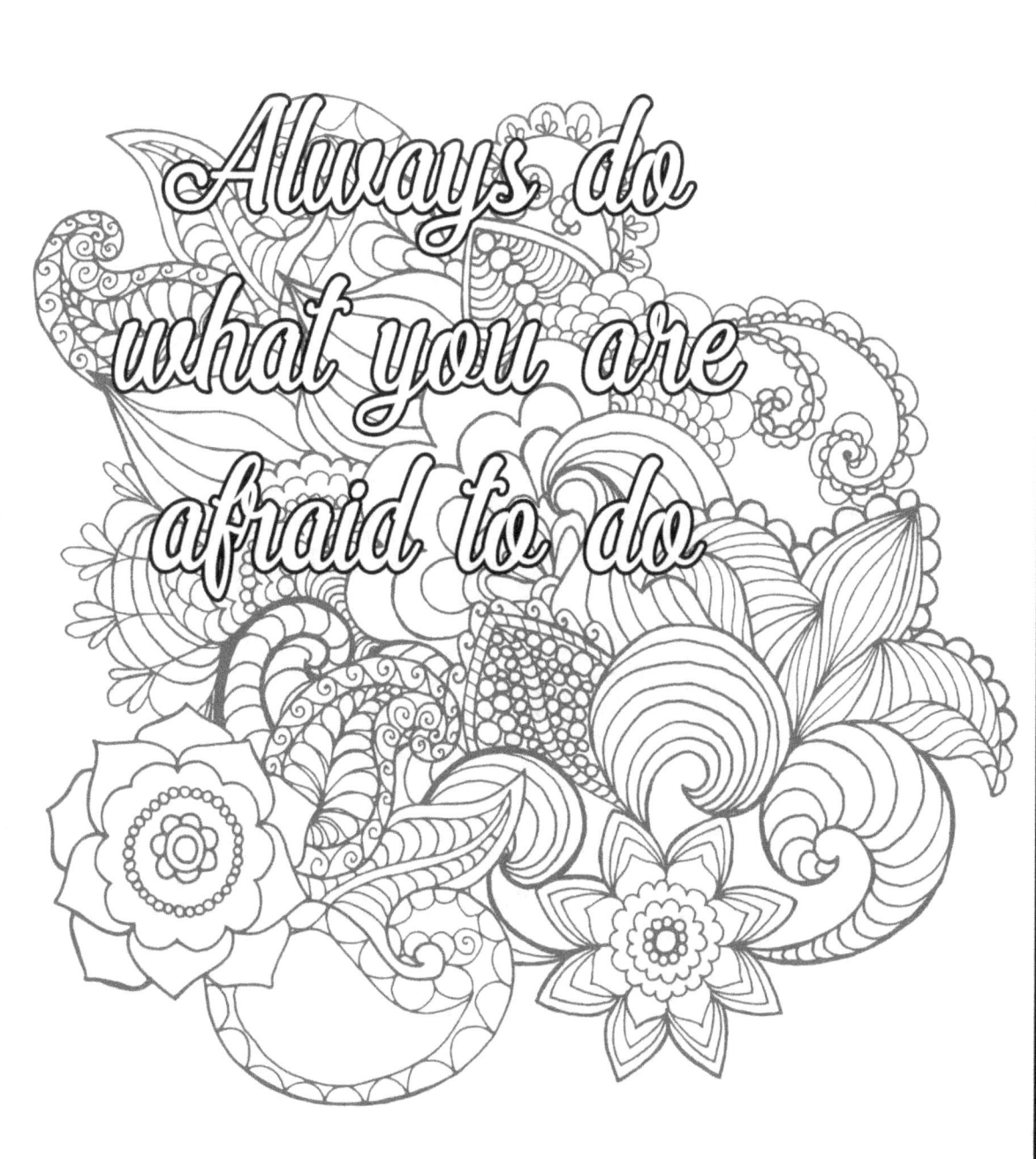

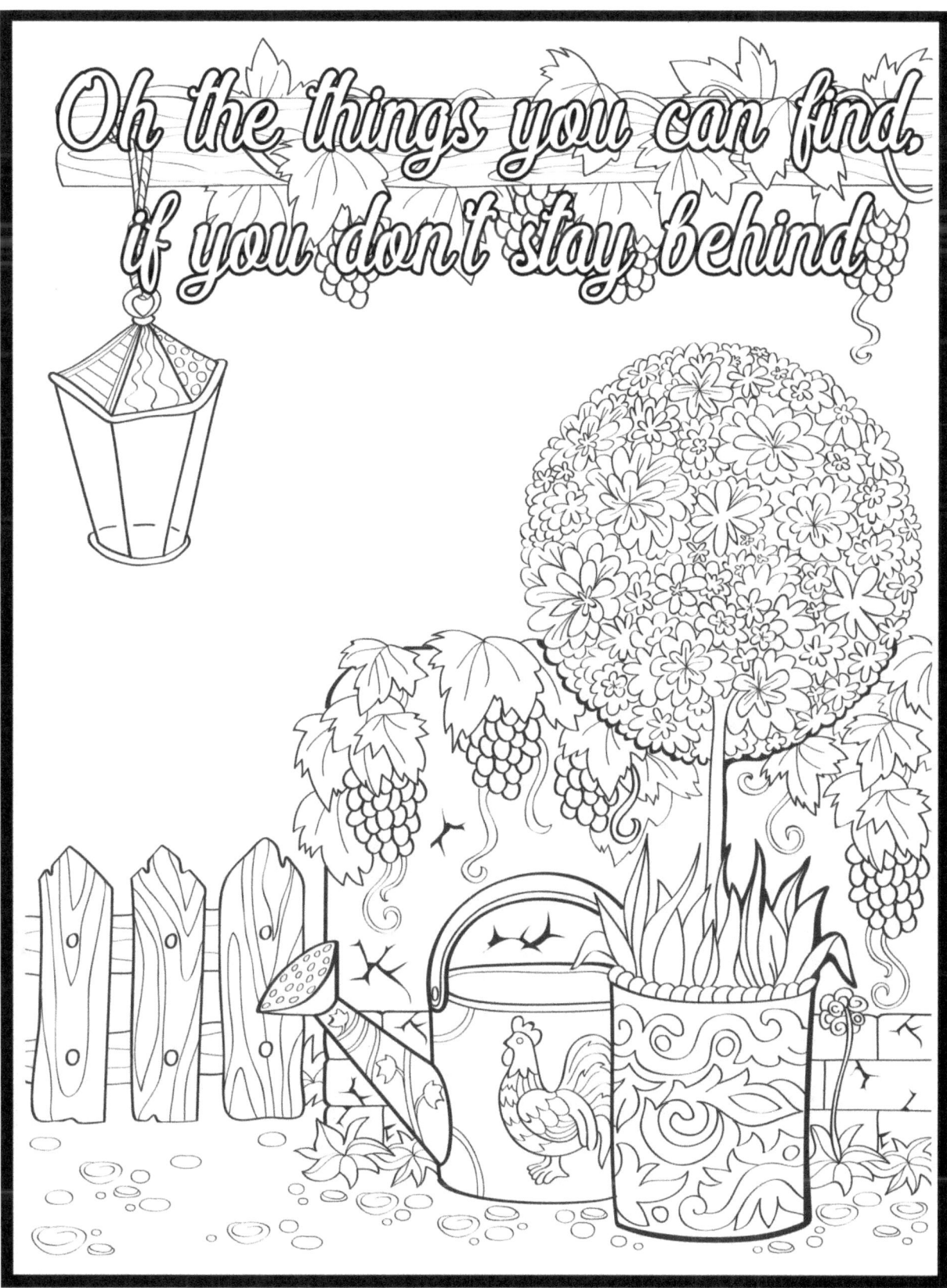

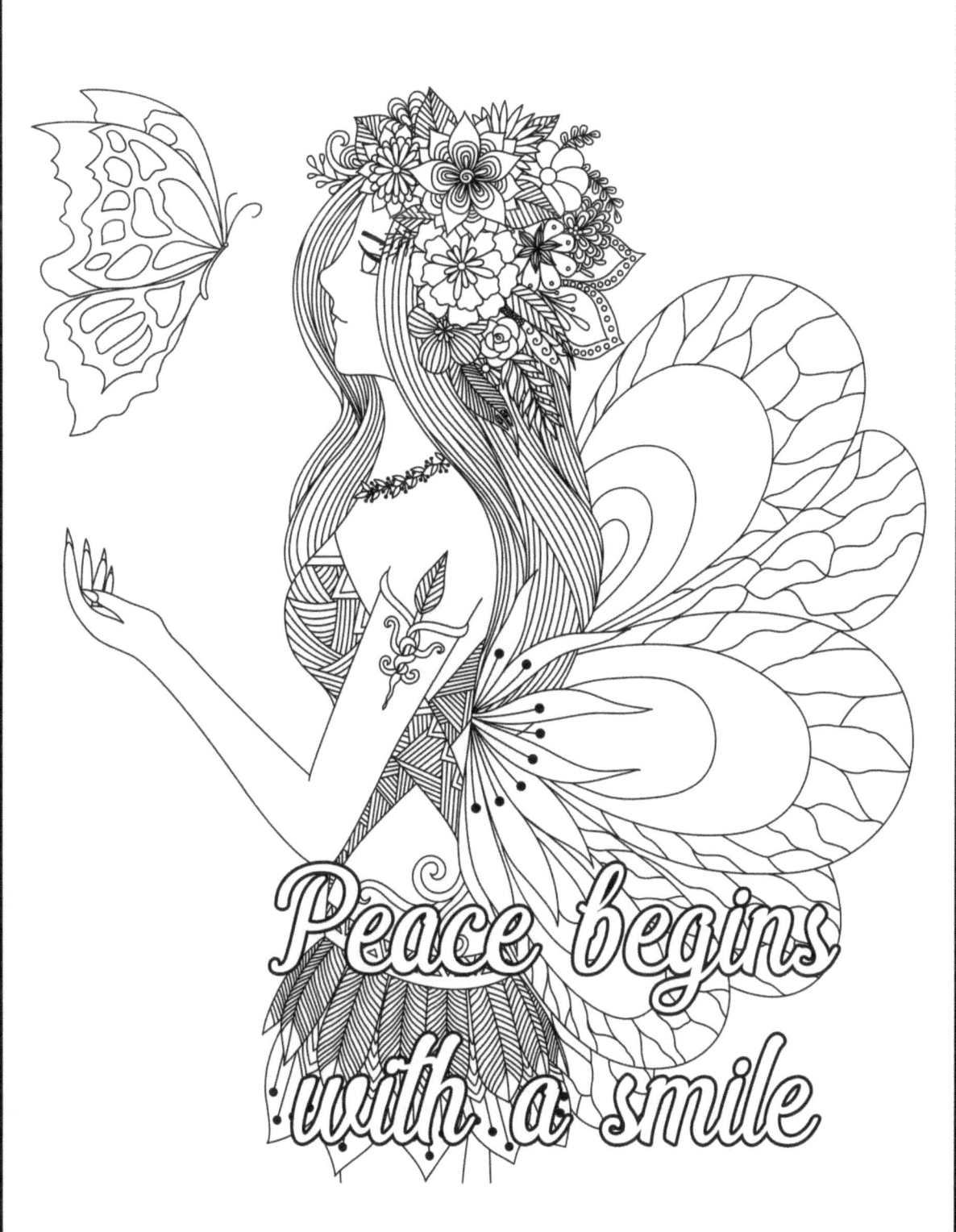

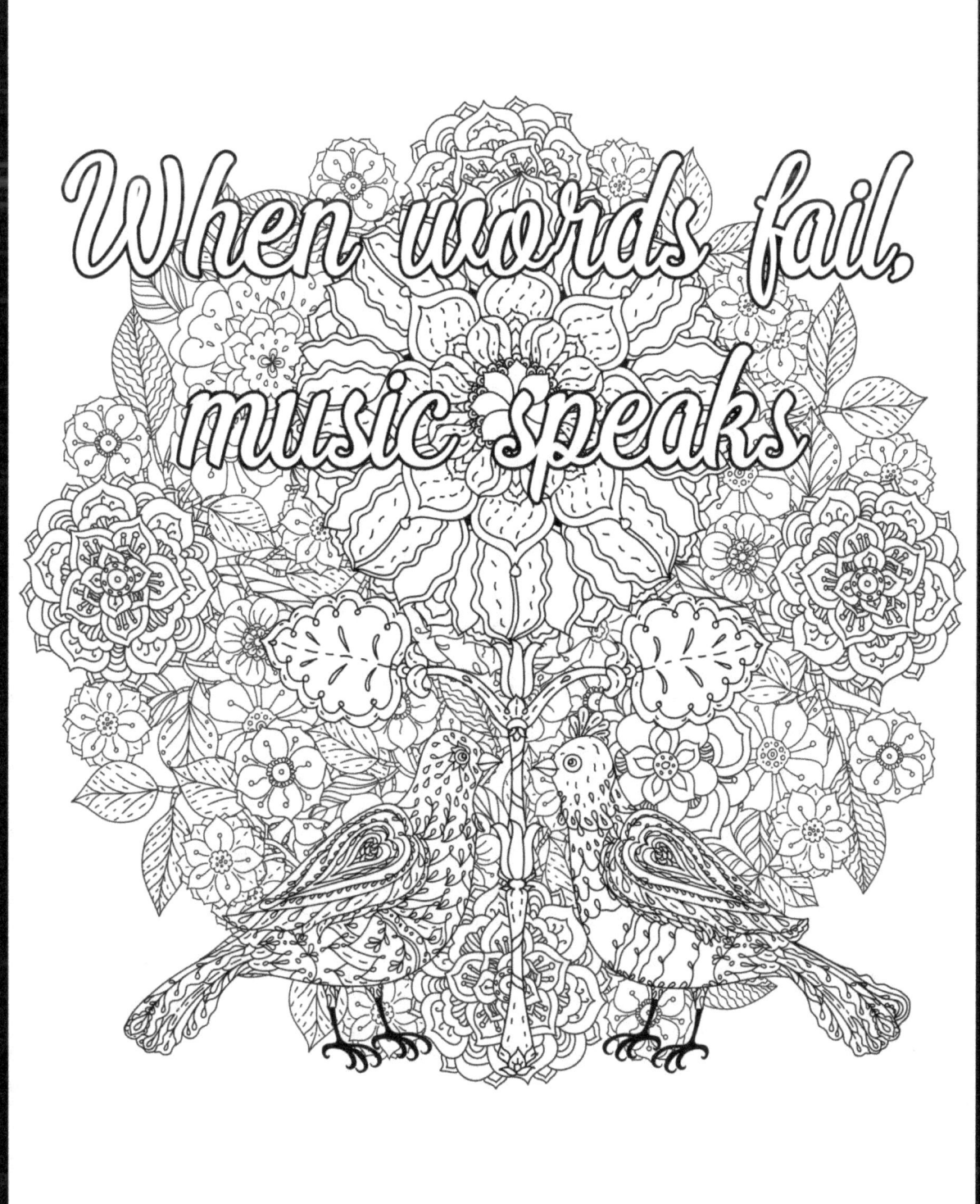

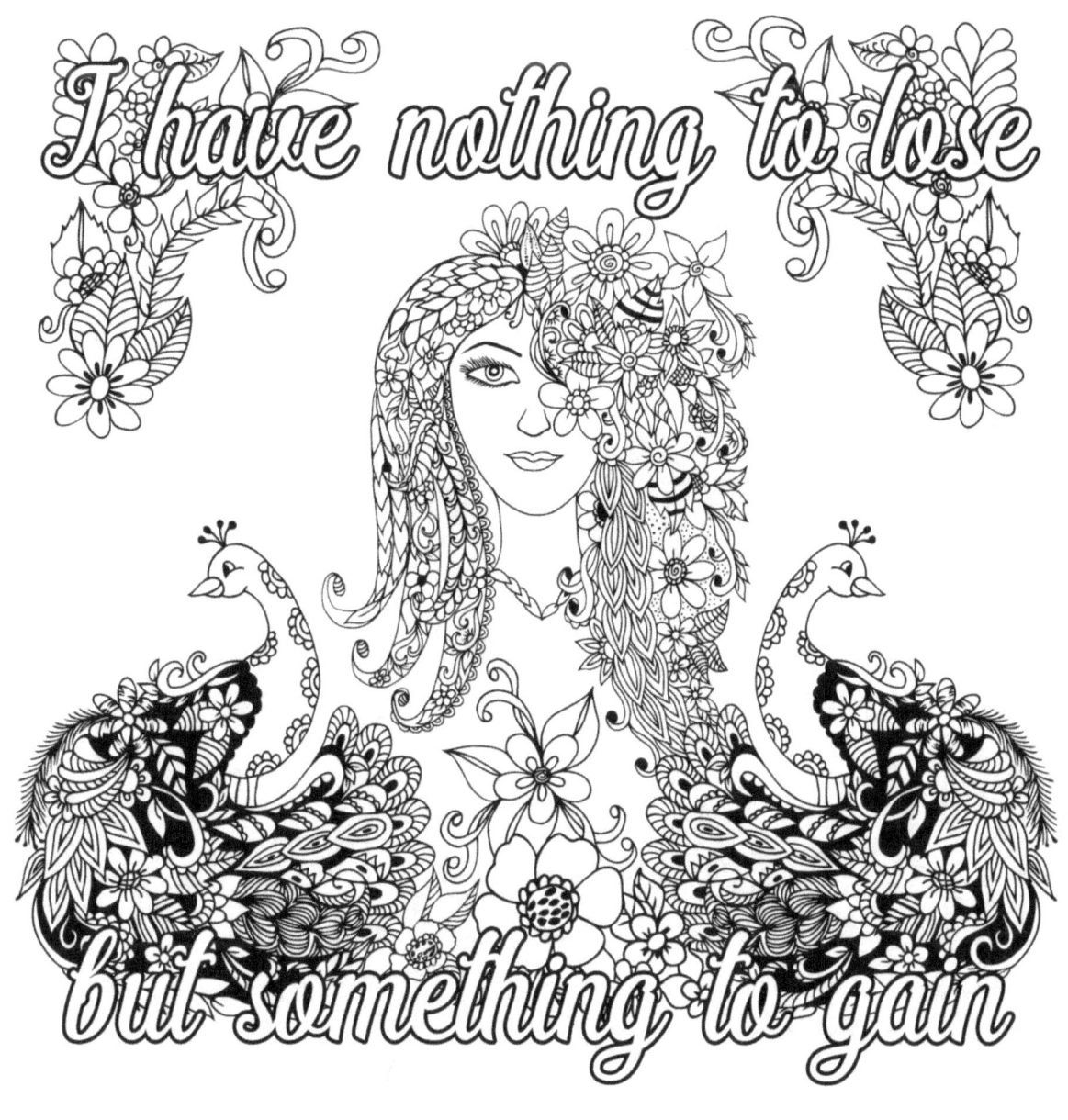

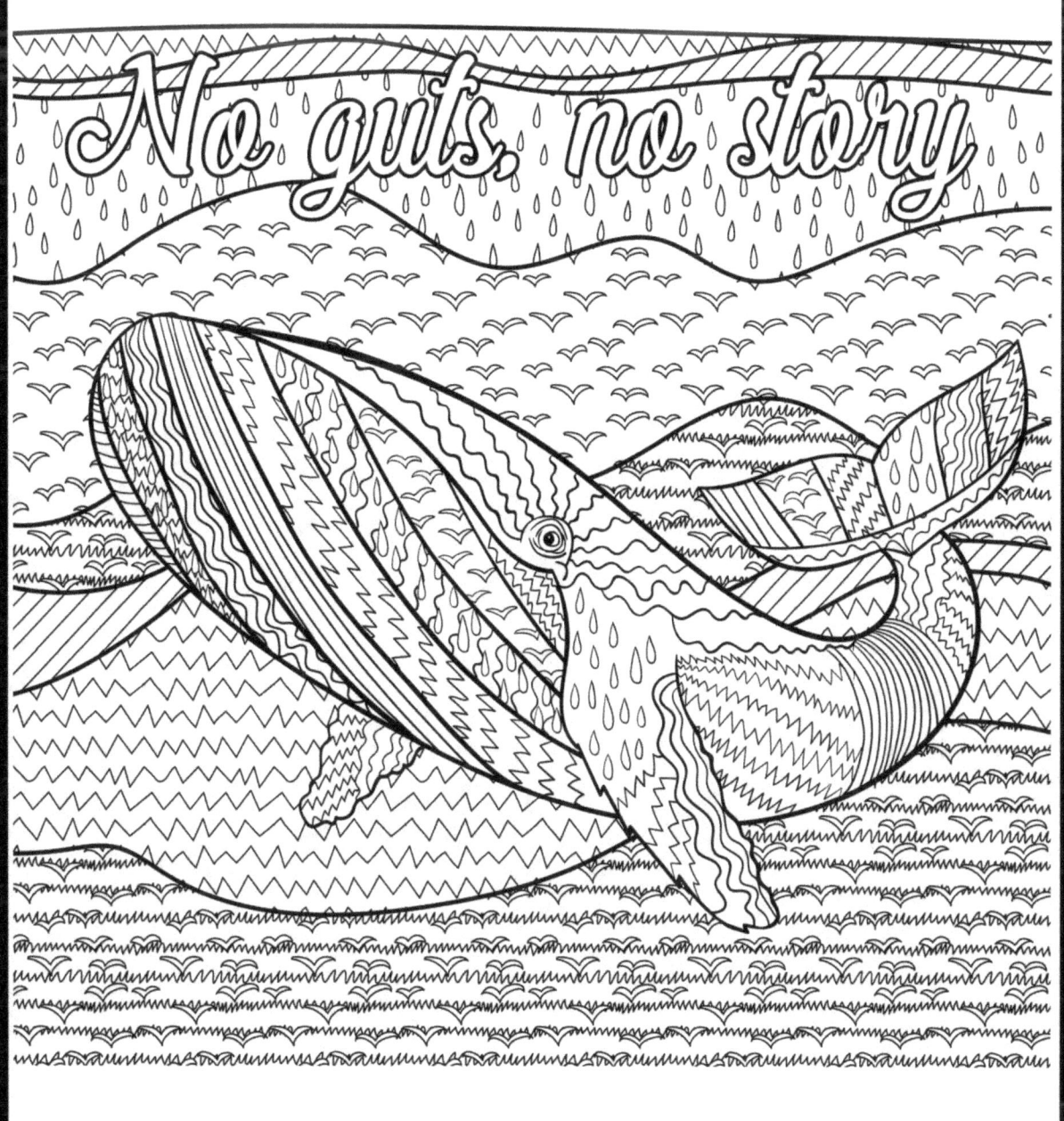

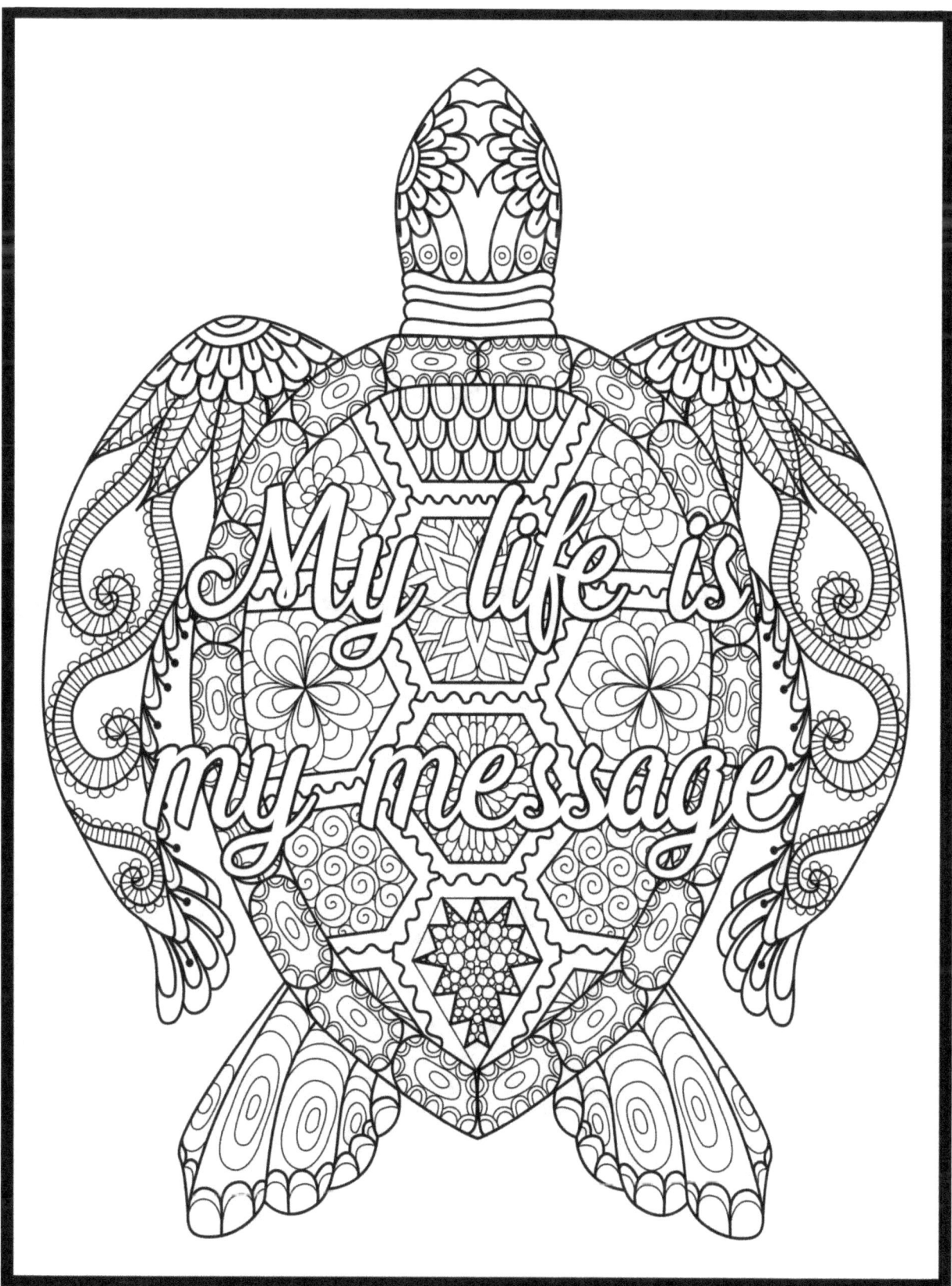

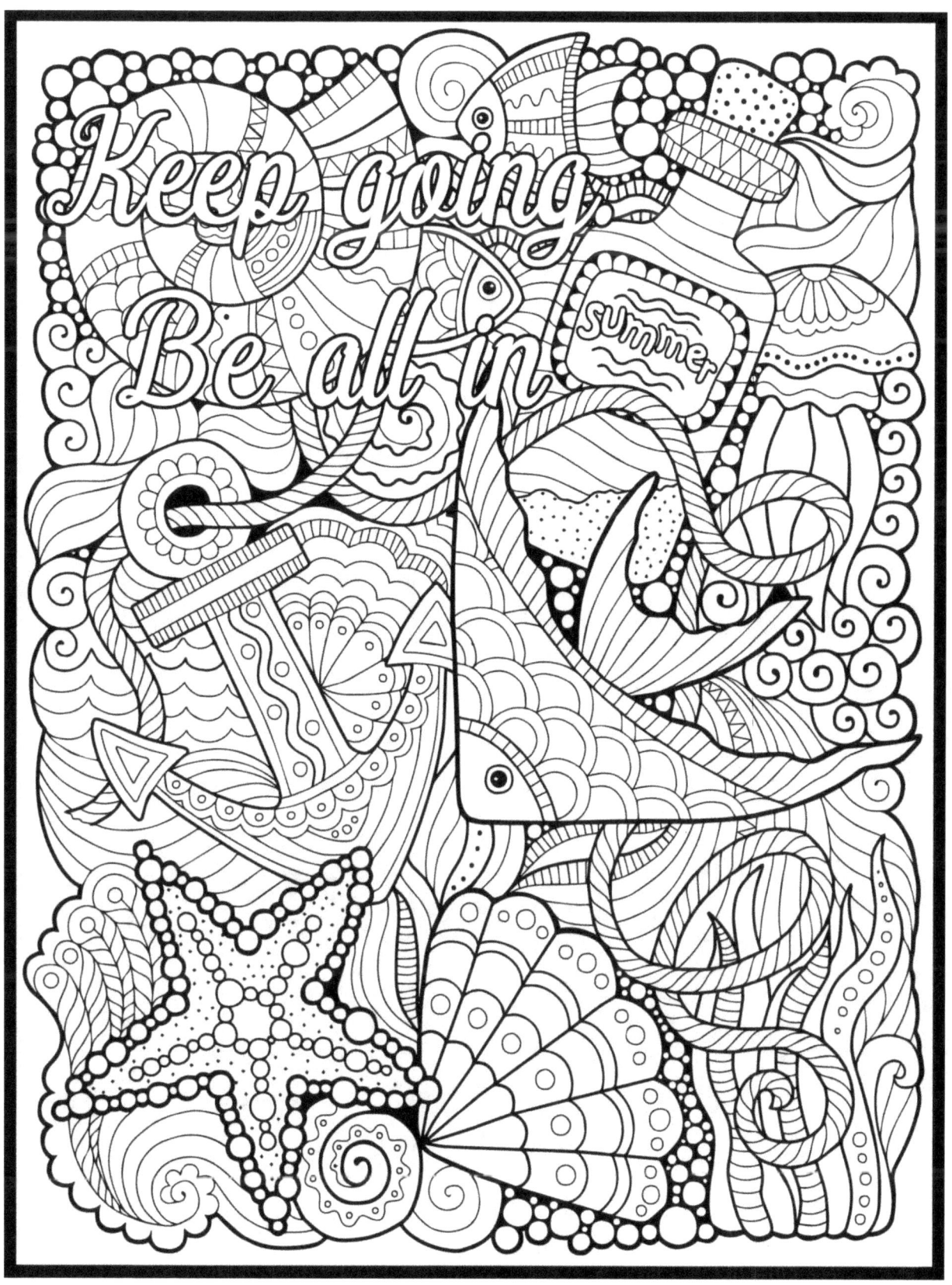

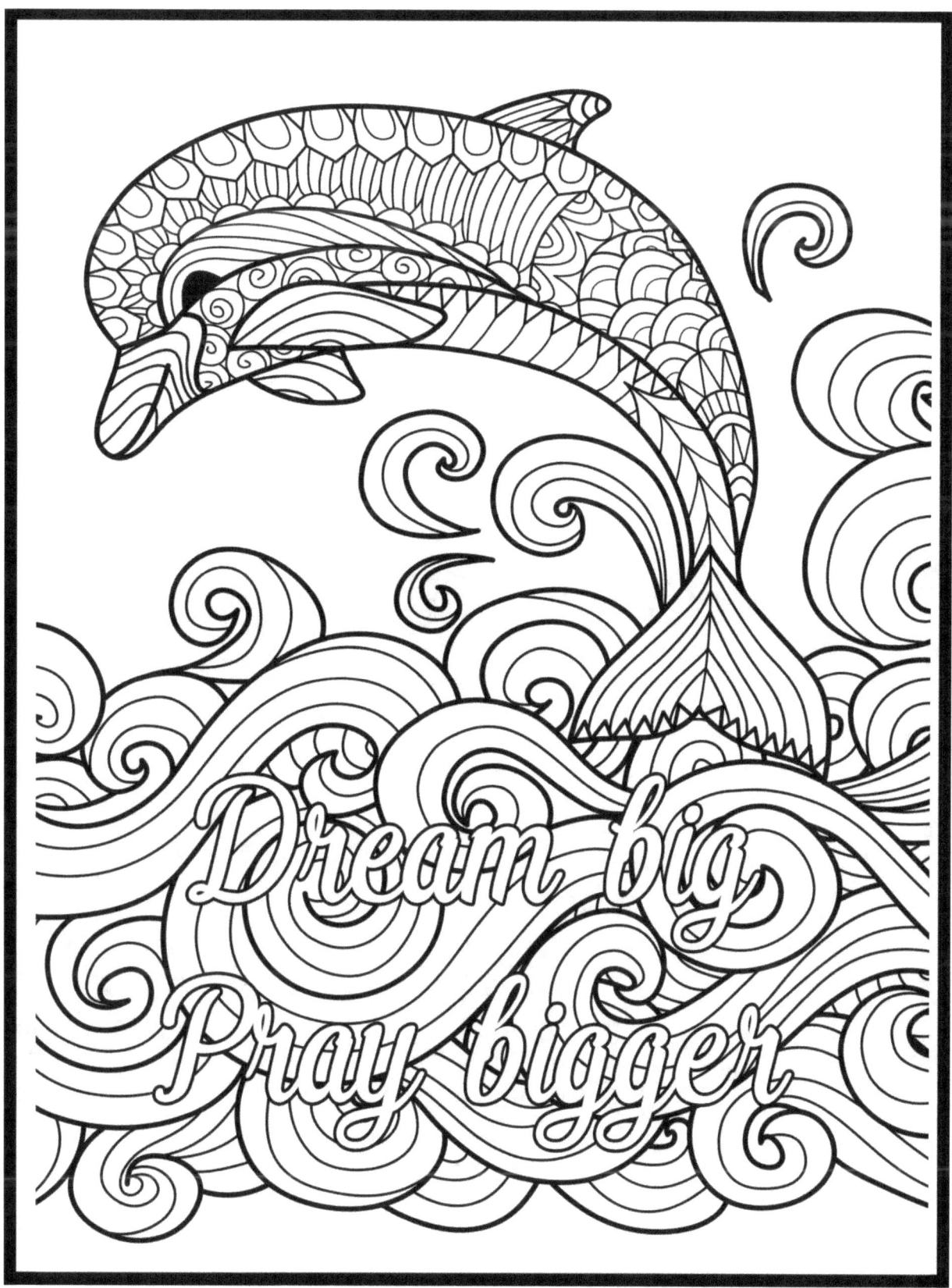

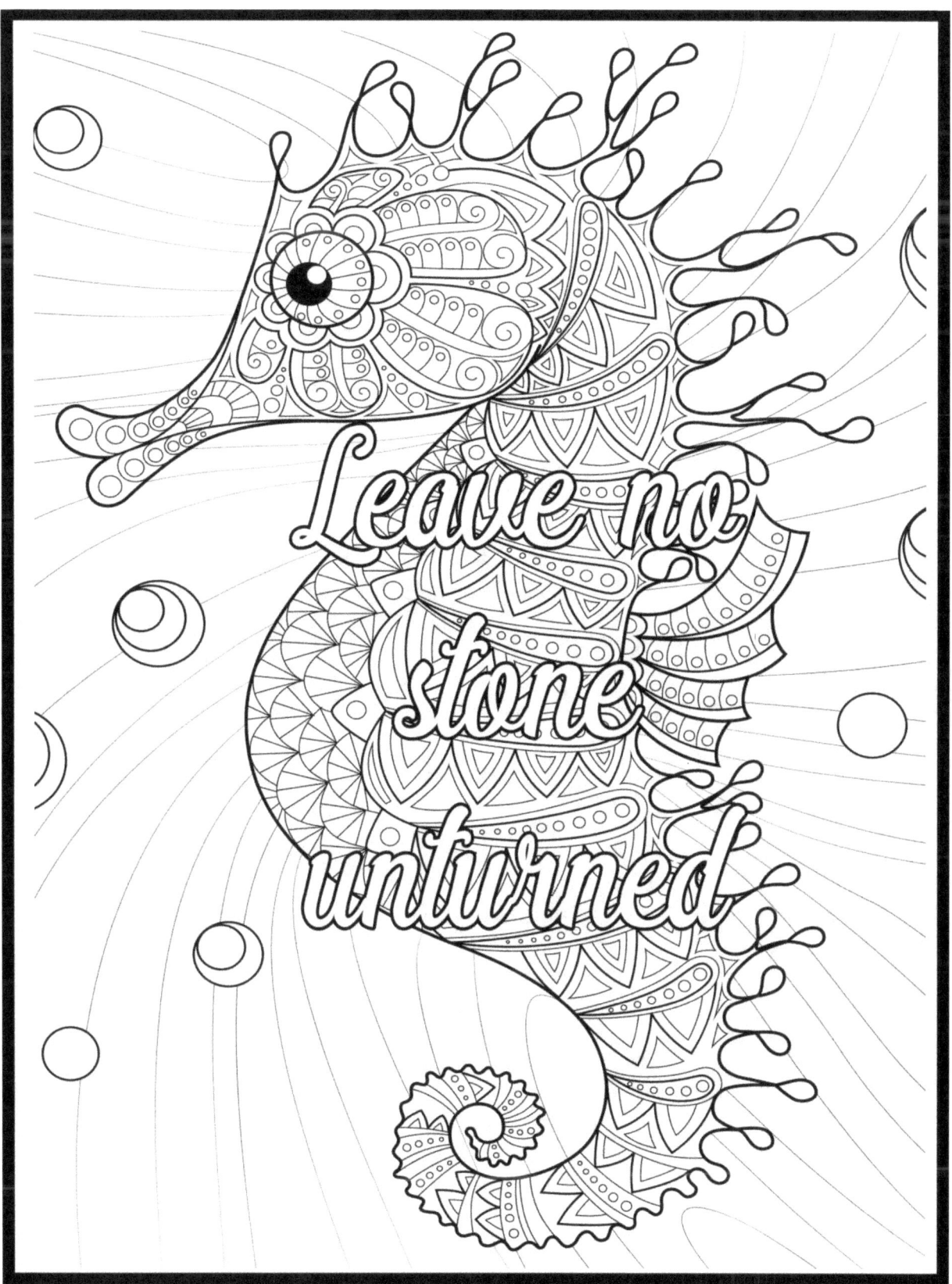

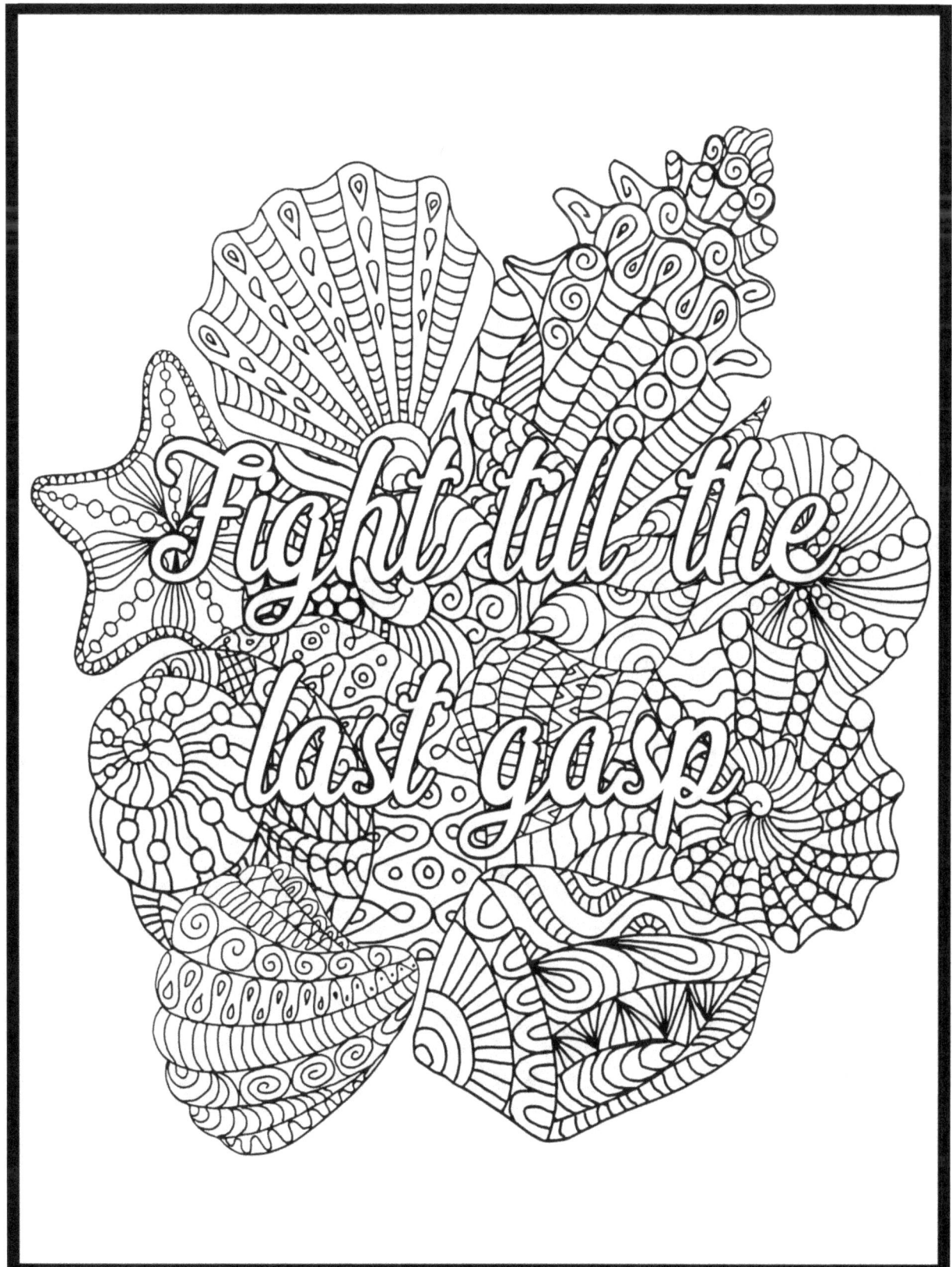

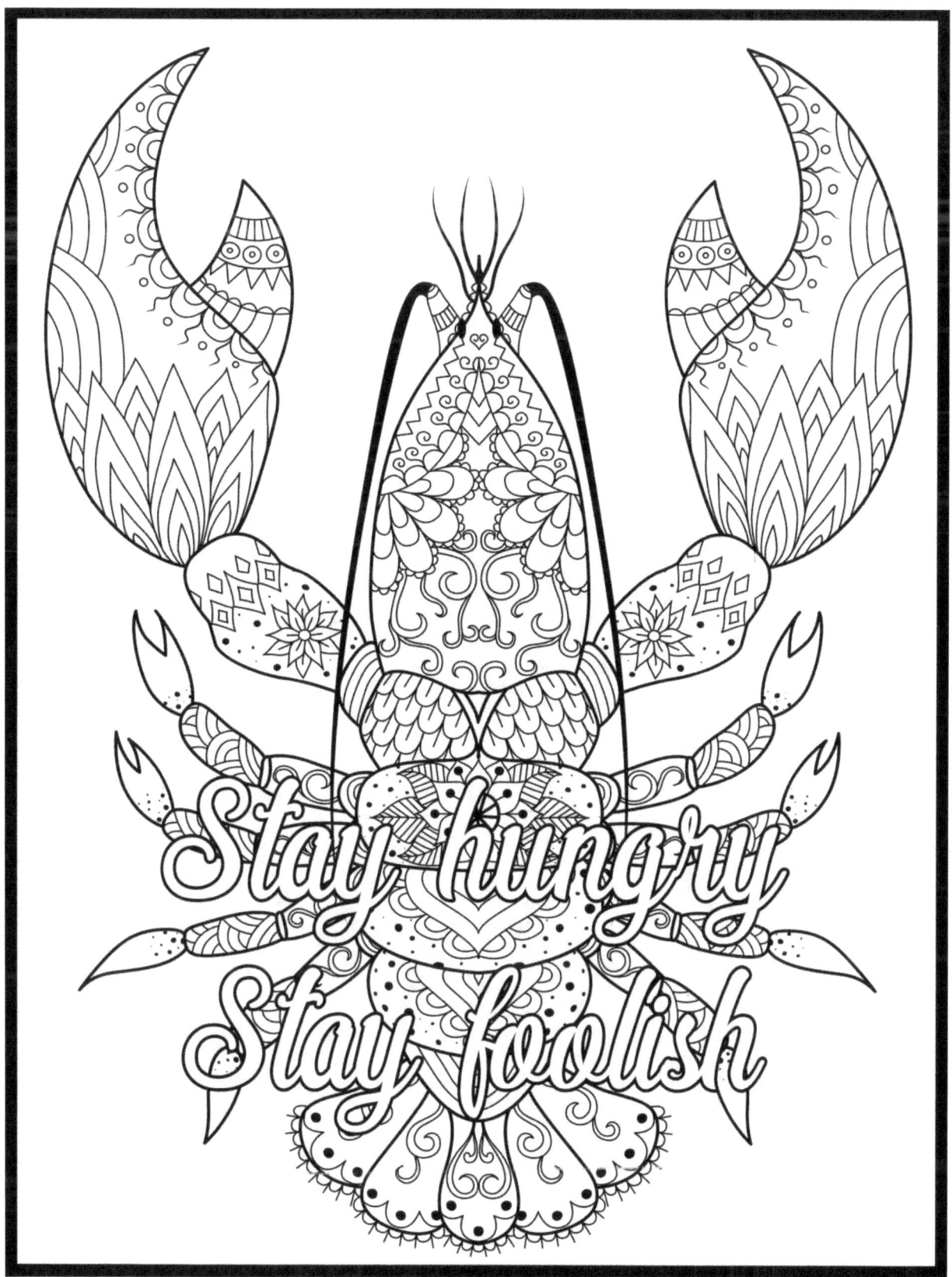

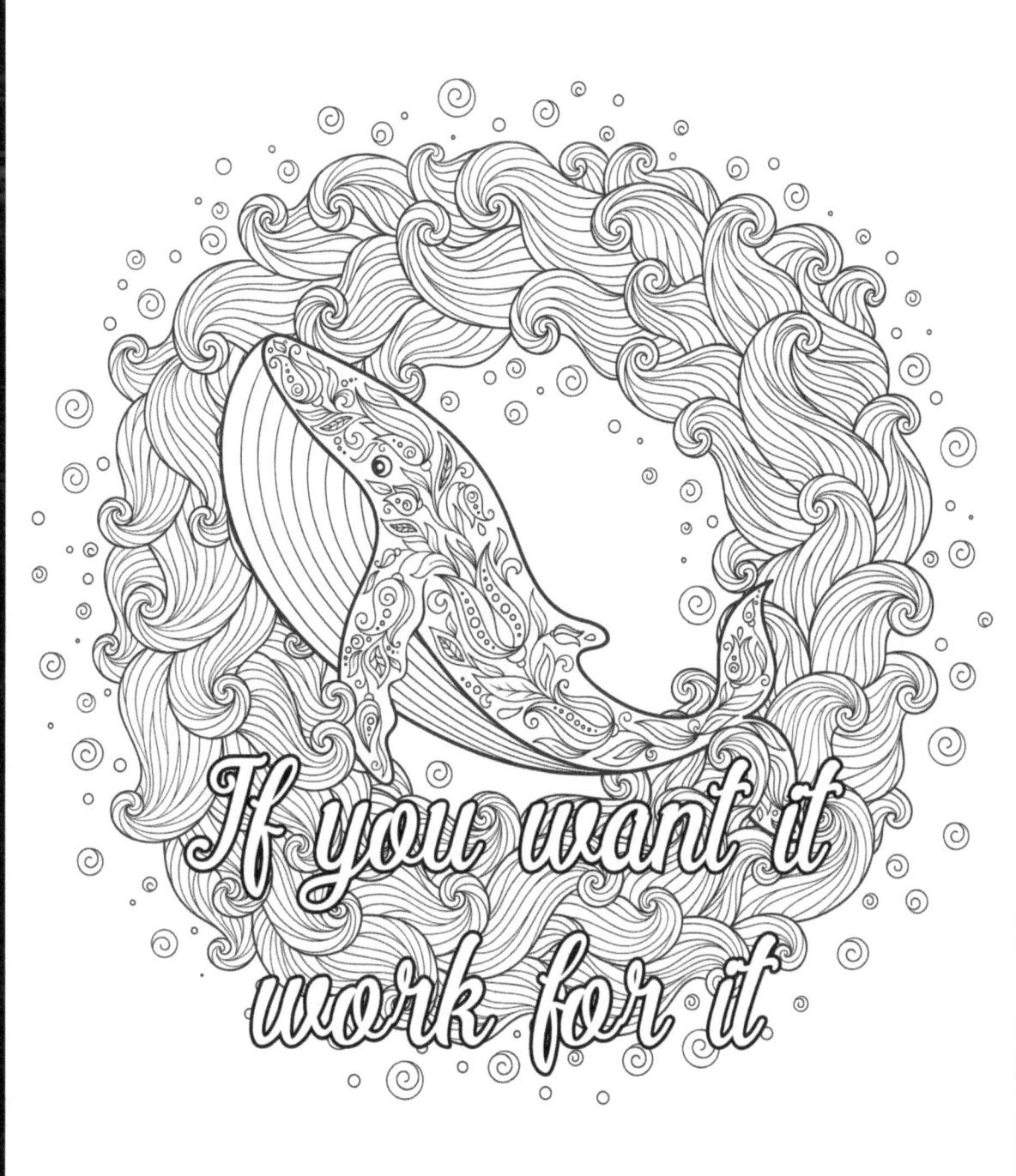

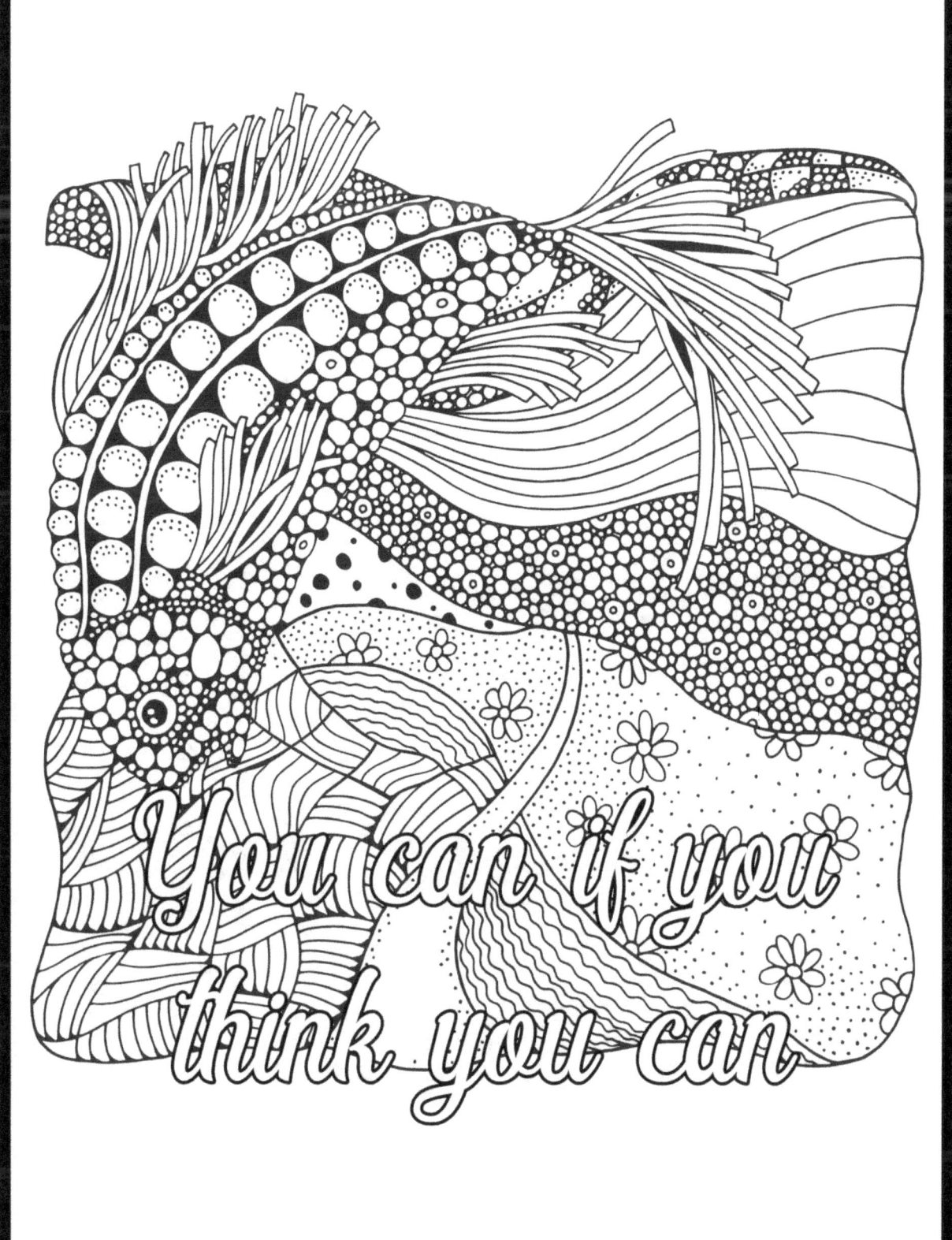

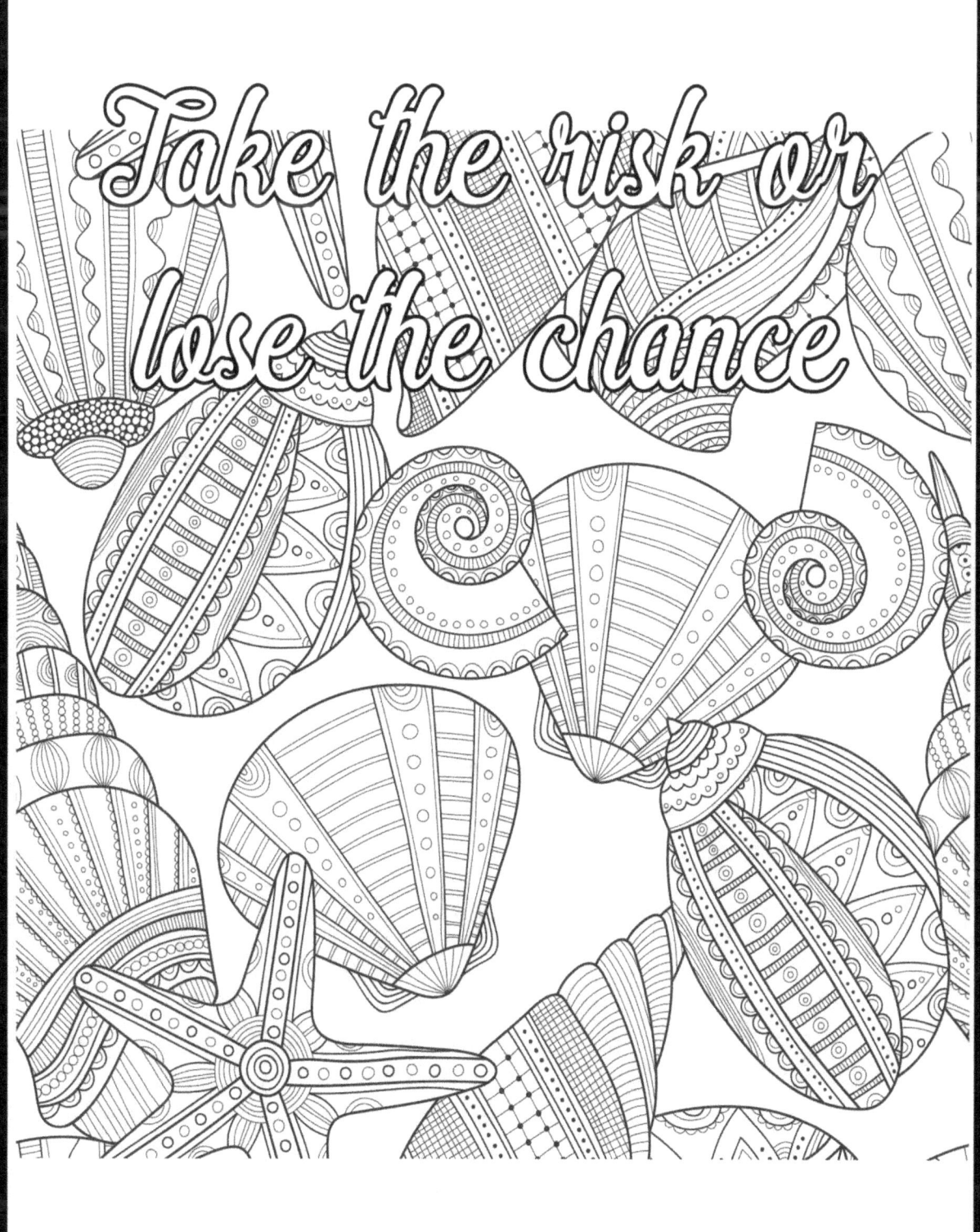

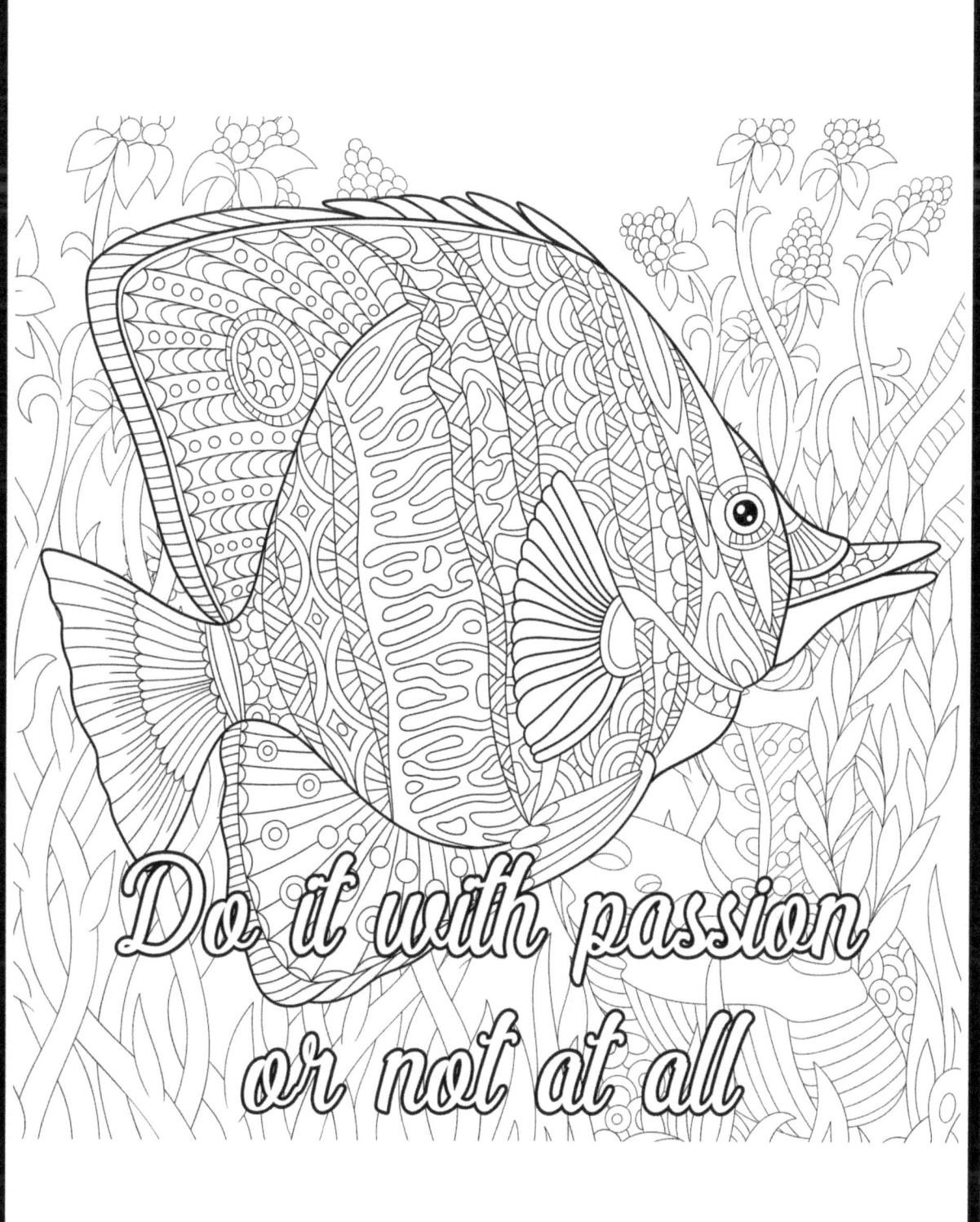

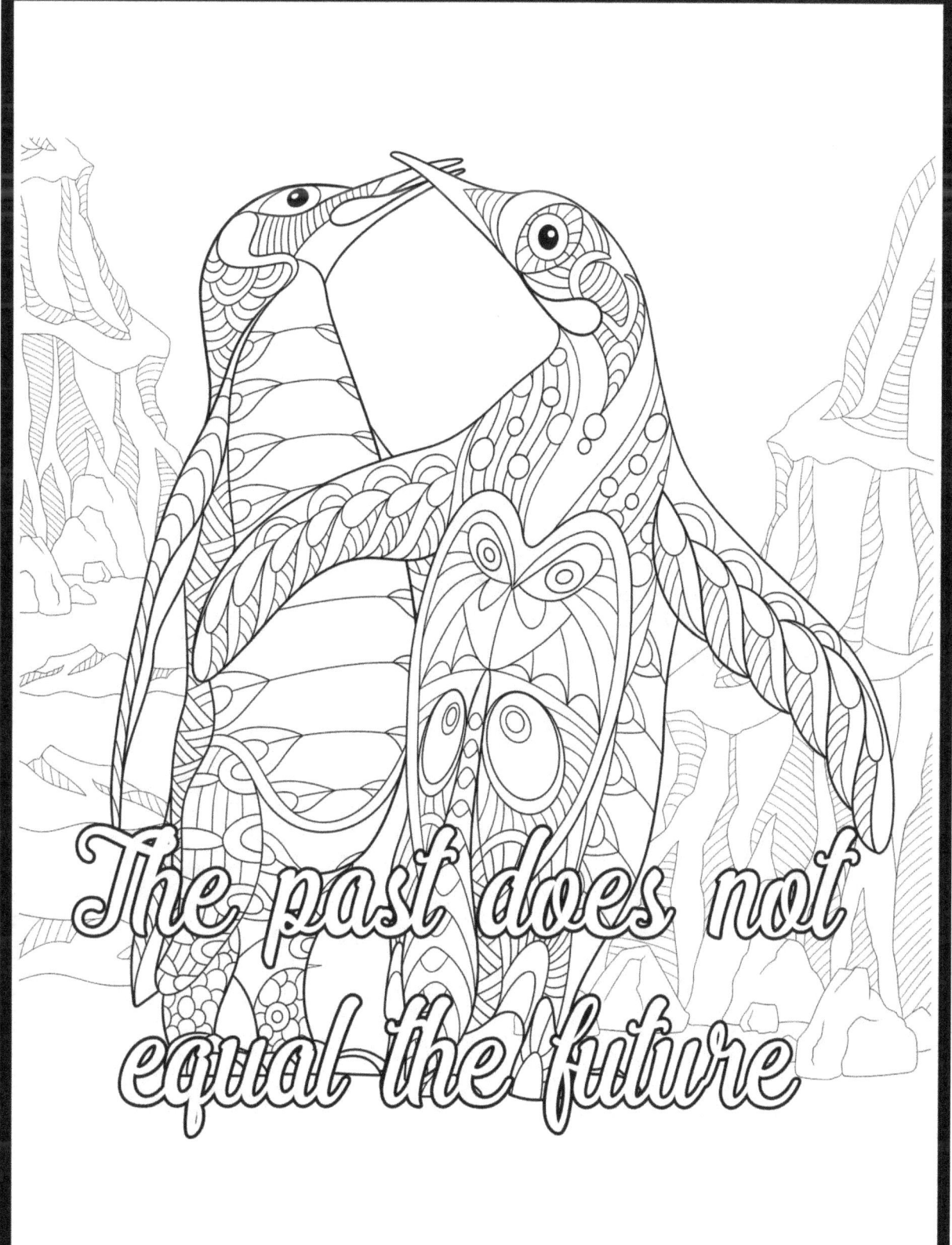

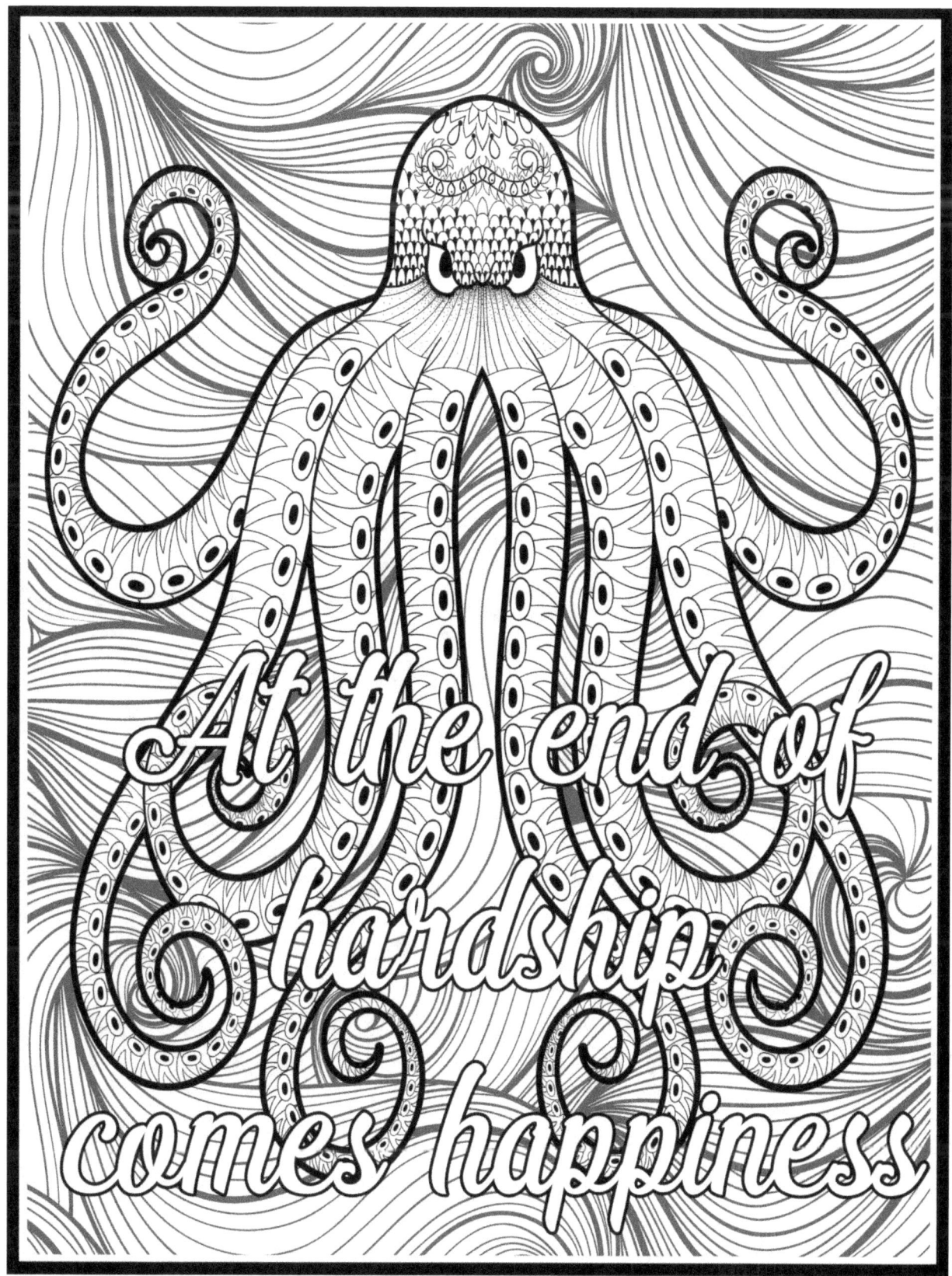

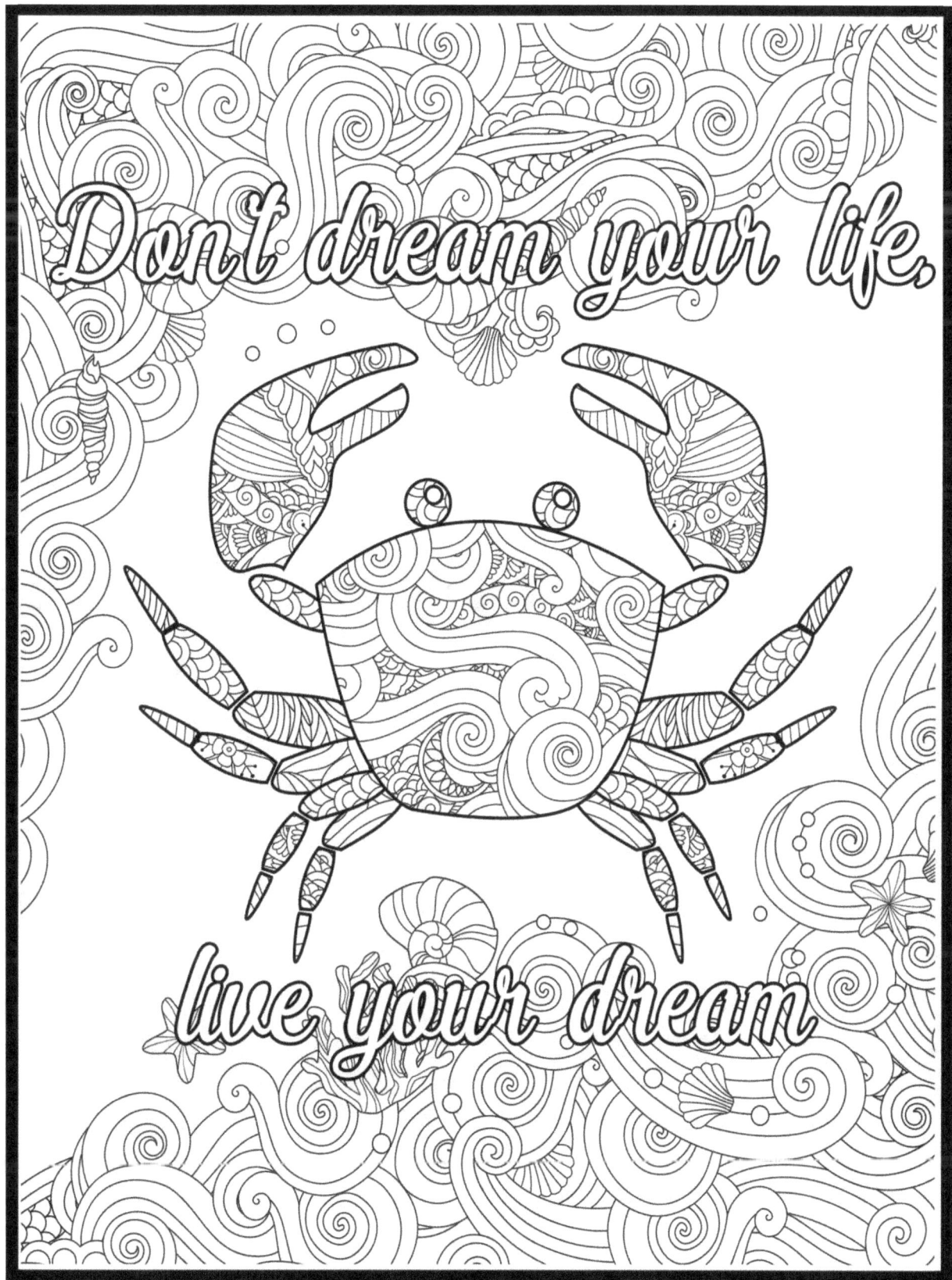

Dream without fear

Love without limits

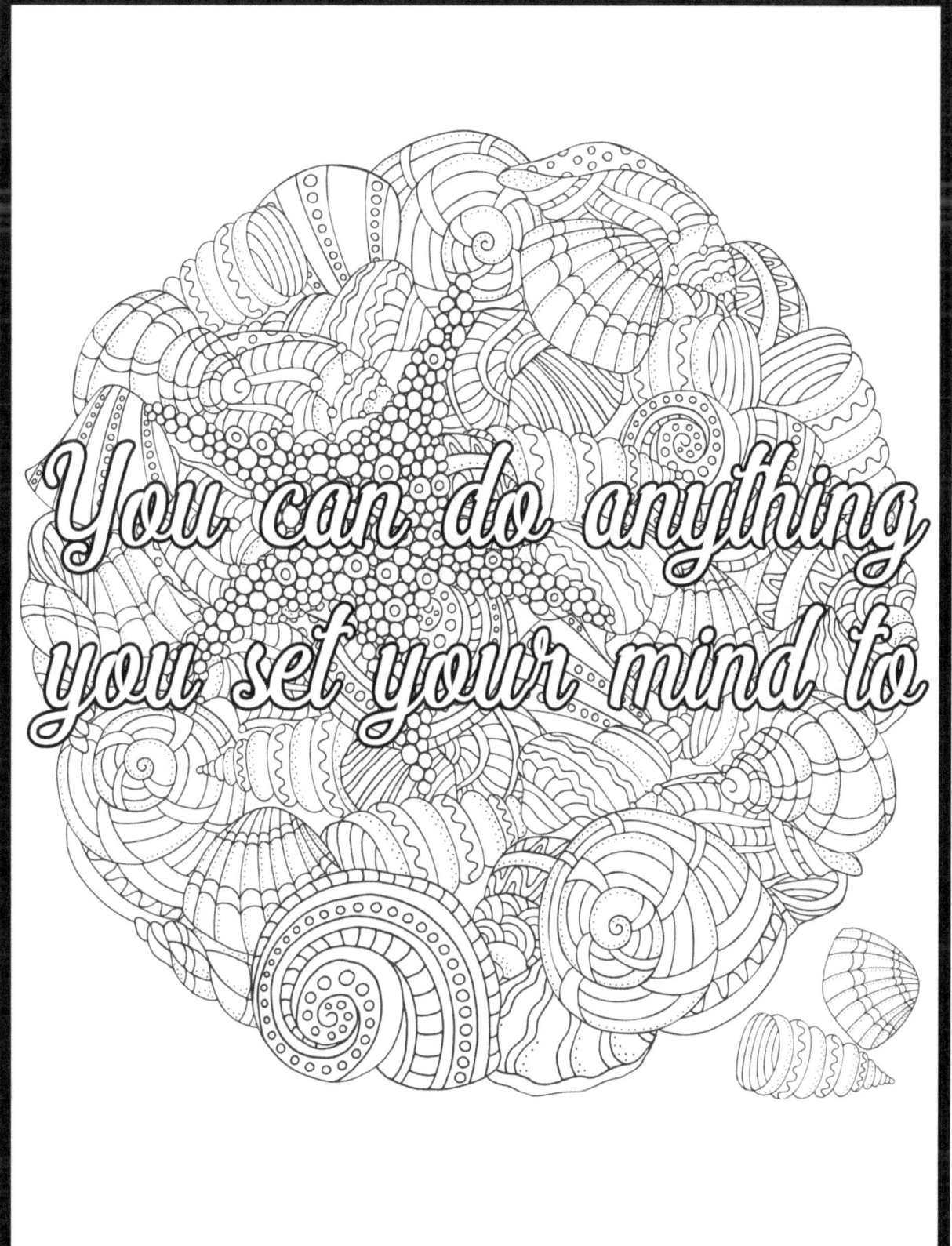

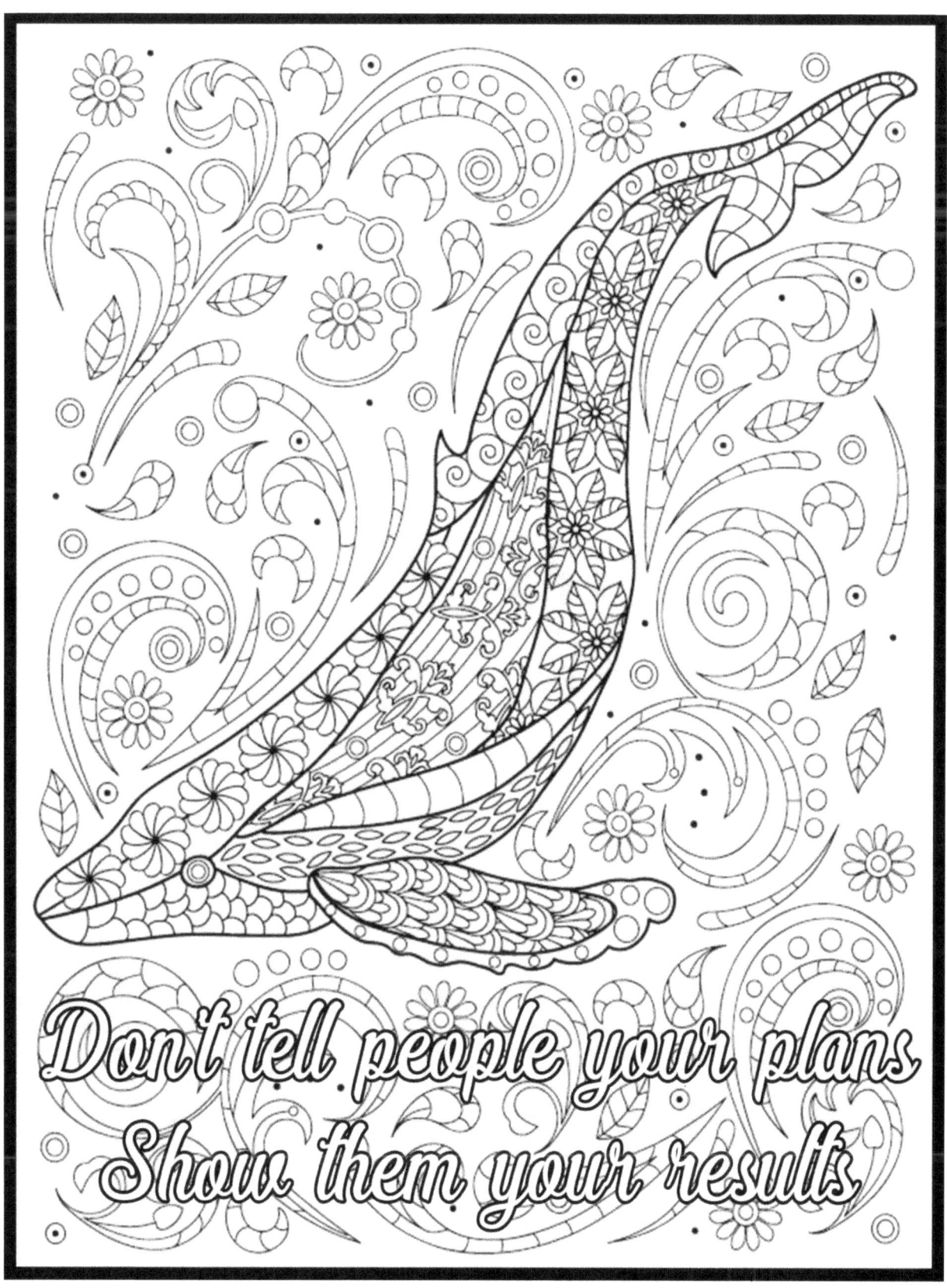

Don't tell people your plans
Show them your results

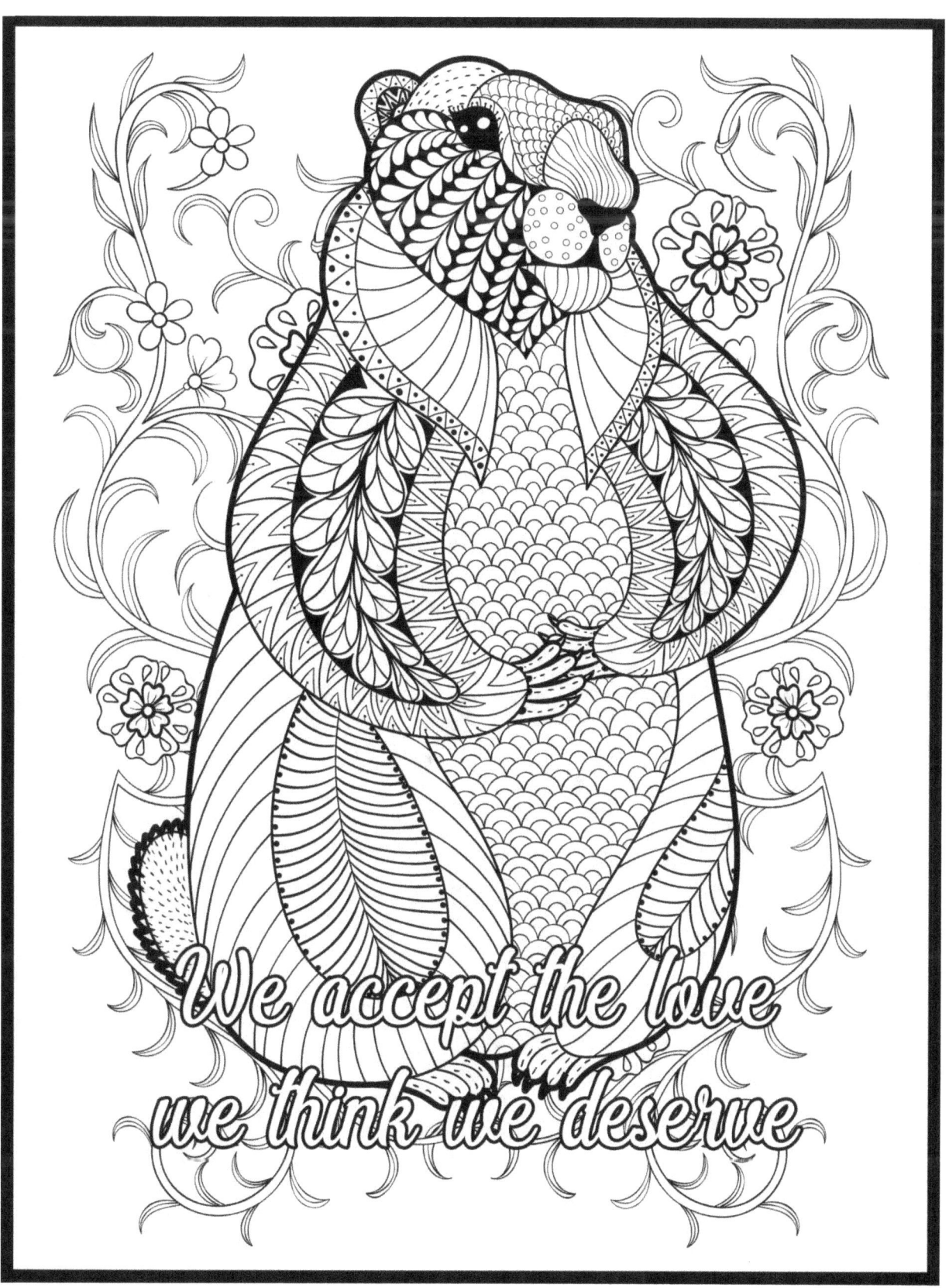

We accept the love
we think we deserve

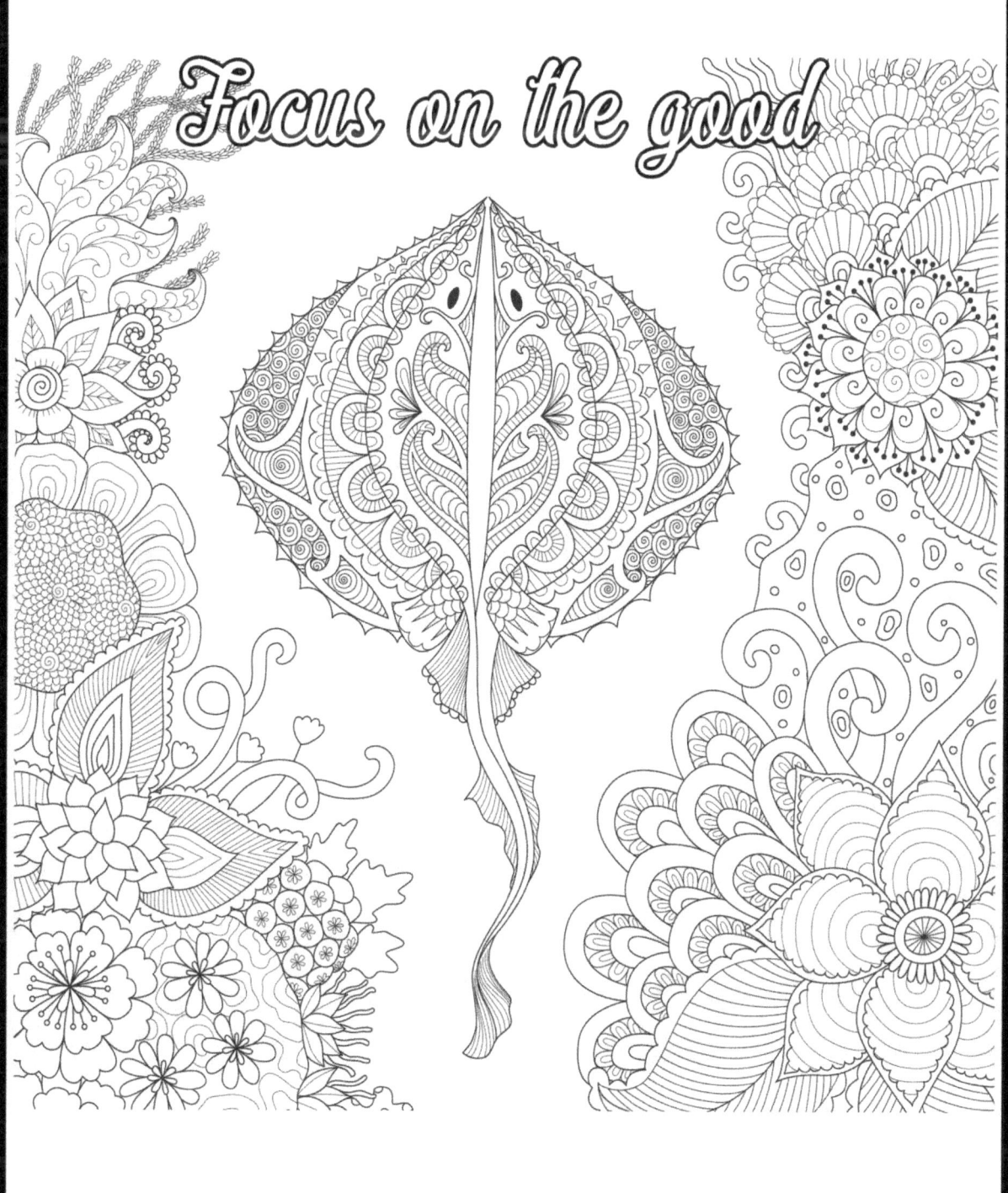

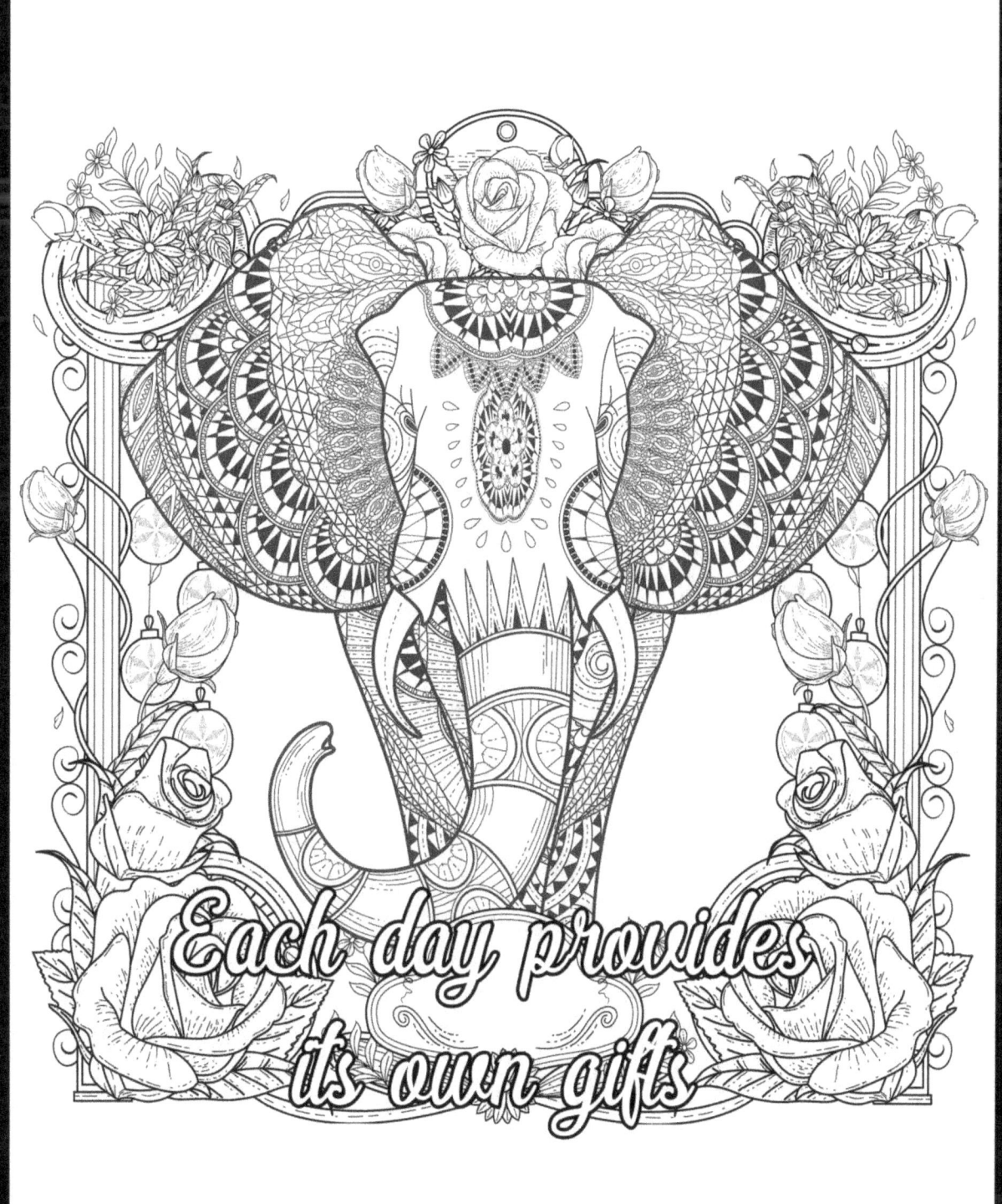

Each day provides its own gifts

www.ingramcontent.com/pod-product-compliance
Lightning Source LLC
Chambersburg PA
CBHW081607220526
45468CB00010B/2800